D'AZUR

MENTON
8

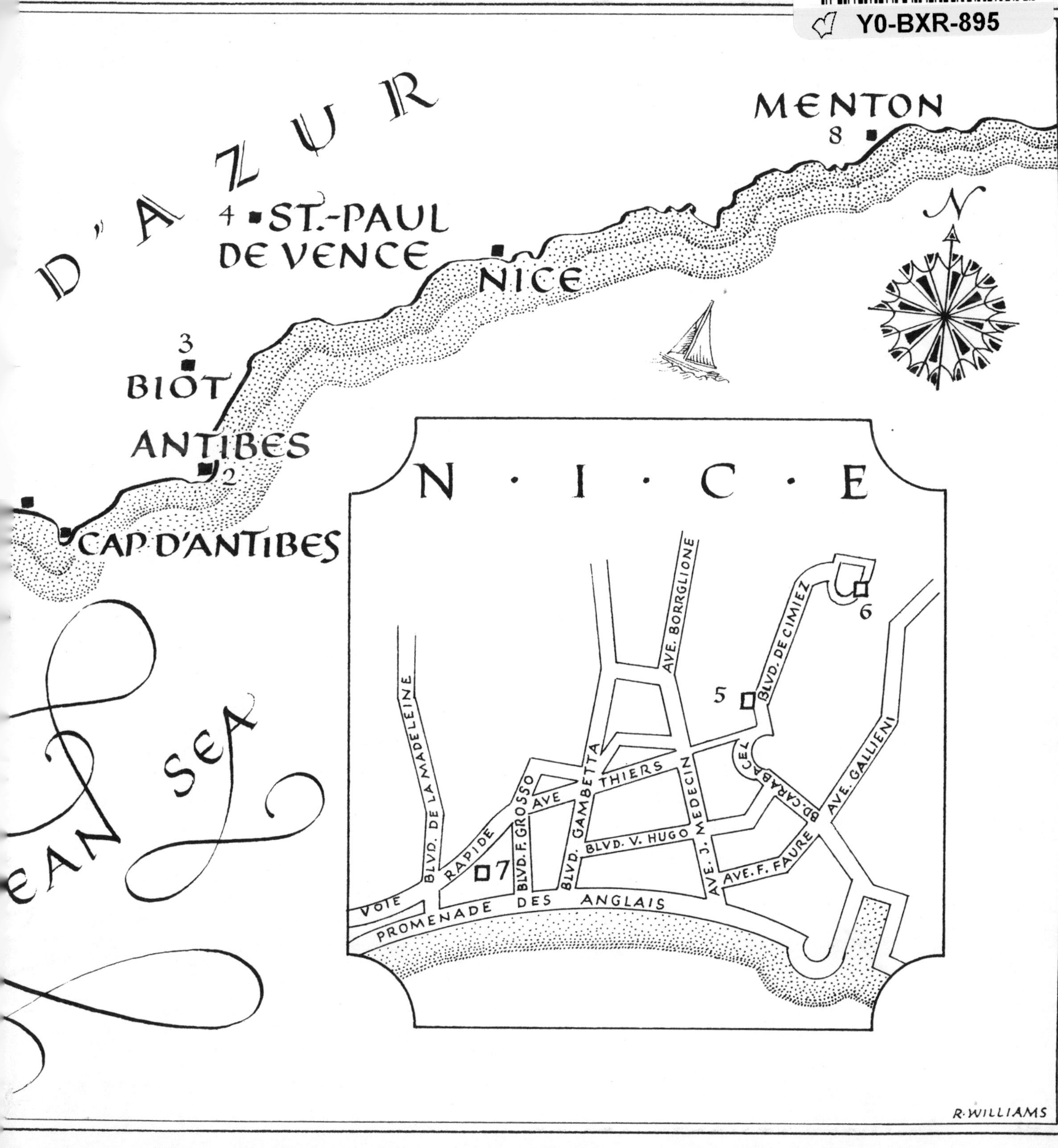

4 ST.-PAUL
DE VENCE

NICE

N

3
BIOT

ANTIBES
2

CAP D'ANTIBES

SEA

EAN

N · I · C · E

AVE. BORRGLIONE

BLVD. DE CIMIEZ

5

6

BLVD. DE LA MADELEINE

VOIE RAPIDE

BLVD. F. GROSSO

AVE. GAMBETTA

THIERS

BLVD. V. HUGO

AVE. J. MEDECIN

BD. CARABACEL

AVE. GALLIENI

AVE. F. FAURE

7

PROMENADE DES ANGLAIS

R. WILLIAMS

MUSEUMS DISCOVERED

Museums of the Côte d'Azur

Thanks are due to Brenda Rendòn, Gordon H. Roberton,
G. Bauquier, Danièle Bourgois, Eric Hild, Patrick Ducournau,
J.G. Martial-Salm, and R. Gianangelli for their participation
and assistance in the publication of this book.

Edited by Leslie Shore

ISBN: 0-9605574-0-7
Library of Congress Card Catalog Number: 80-84917

Created for Penshurst Books, Inc. by
Shorewood Fine Art Books
475 Tenth Avenue
New York, N.Y. 10018

MUSEUMS DISCOVERED

Museums of the Côte d'Azur

Penshurst Books
Fort Lee, New Jersey

Created by Shorewood Fine Art Books, New York

Introduction

The Côte d'Azur in the south of France is one of the most splendid coastlines of the West. Its very name conjures up an image of the Riviera, the blue Mediterranean, white beaches, and a life of luxury. The towns ranged along its shores, bathed in a strong meridional sunlight, have become centers of tourism and art. There is a prestigious international film festival in Cannes; every year Nice sponsors a vast Mardi Gras celebration, and the casinos of Monte Carlo are legendary. While the Côte d'Azur can be said to stretch from Marseilles to Menton at the Italian border, covering the Département des Alpes-Maritimes, its heart is a strip of coast running from St.-Tropez to Menton.

The district is far older than most casual visitors would guess. Marseilles was settled as early as 600 B.C. by Greek traders, who built a large port there and named it Massilia; many of the other cities of the Côte d'Azur were also founded in Classical times. Throughout the Middle Ages and the Renaissance these port towns continued to function; battlements and fortifications have been preserved that testify to the many wars that swept the area in those centuries. But it was in the grand era of the Baroque and the gracious decades of the Rococo that the Côte d'Azur developed its present character. At that time, many palaces and villas were built to accommodate the aristocracy during the winter months. The nineteenth and twentieth centuries have contributed to the flowering of this district as a resort; the season for vacationers is no longer only a few months long, but lasts all year.

Before the Riviera was the elegant resort area we see now, it was the haunt of artists. The appeal of the Côte d' Azur for them was manifold. It was an inexpensive place to live, and the warm climate drew many of them from northern cities. But there are other, more fundamental reasons why so many artists chose to work there. In the middle years of the nineteenth century, landscapists came to record the beauties of the seashore. Later, the Post-Impressionists, especially the Divisionists, interested in studying the effects of refracted light, were drawn by the brilliant sunlight and colors of the Midi. Artists like Dufy, who wished to record the pageant of society, came to depict the gracious boulevards, casinos, and racetracks of Nice and Monte Carlo. Picasso came south after the Second World War to discover both the lingering antiquity of Antibes and the daily life of its fishing community. Léger, impressed by the ceramic traditions of Biot, set up his own studio there.

Their activity did not go unnoticed. Collectors began to buy their art and to establish museums in many of these towns. This in turn encouraged the artists and their families to donate their works to the public, creating many small museums to honor the works of a single artist. Given the modest scale of these museums and the extremely sophisticated patronage and connoisseurship that support them, each one has acquired a distinctive personality. They are characterized by the individual taste of a collector or the unique aesthetic of an artist. This individuality is further reinforced by the buildings that house these collections; they range from renovated chapels to grand châteaux to unique examples of modern architecture. While it cannot include every collection in an area so rich in art (there are over thirty museums in the Côte d'Azur district), this volume introduces some of the finest of these museums and their magnificent possessions.

Musée de l'Annonciade, St.-Tropez

Built in 1568, the old Chapel of the Annunciation of St.-Tropez was transformed into a museum by the art patron Georges Grammont, aided by the architect André Barbier-Bouvet, who designed a new first floor in 1937. In opening this museum, Grammont was continuing and expanding a 1922 project of Henri Person and André Turin. At the instigation of Signac and with the generosity of their painter friends who had worked at St.-Tropez, these two patrons of the arts had been able to bring together some thirty canvases. This seminal collection was assembled by the municipality and shown in a room of the Town Hall. It was first called the *Museon Tropelen*.

With the approval of the Direction des Beaux-Arts of the town, Grammont soon enlarged the collection with a group of works representative of modern French painting, including some by Marquet, Matisse, Manguin, Ranson, and Vallotton.

After the Second World War, Grammont was anxious to complete the project he had started. In 1950, he planned an expansion of the museum, and he obtained permission from the municipality of St.-Tropez to further renovate the Chapel of the Annunciation. The architect Louis Süe was entrusted with the arrangement of the galleries. While respecting the sobriety of the exterior of the building, Süe was able to construct a clear and spacious interior, on a scale that could, in his words, favorably display painting and sculpture "to which all must yield, even the architecture, which should serve and not interfere." After five years of close collaboration between Süe and Grammont, the Musée de l'Annonciade was inaugurated on July 10, 1955. The installation was directed by the three curators of the new museum, Grammont, Süe, and the artist André Dunoyer de Segonzac.

Grammont died in 1956. In 1955, he had given the French government six fine works from his own collection. These were placed in the museum, where today they are hung with important works acquired by the city of St.-Tropez or given to the museum by the French government.

Although the collection is roughly divided between Post-Impressionists and modern French masters, it shows a remarkable overall unity, due to the discerning taste of Grammont. The oldest of the pictures in the museum, bequeathed by the collector, is from 1890; a Divisionist masterpiece by Seurat, it is peculiarly representative of the character of the museum as a whole. Grammont was fascinated with all aspects of the Divisionist revolution. He generally excluded works belonging to the more abstract and conceptual movements of Cubism, Orphism, Dada, and Surrealism, but was receptive to the new forms that emerged from the aesthetic of the Post-Impressionist avant garde.

The collection as a whole is made up of significant works—in many cases, chefs d'oeuvre—of the Divisionists, Nabis, Fauves, and independent artists from the years 1890 to 1950. More recent acquisitions continue to enrich the museum, and it also sponsors special exhibitions and diverse cultural activities. At its heart, the Annonciade museum reflects an artistic outlook which is defined, pertinent, classic, and delicate, in a framework which derives its force from its subtle aesthetic unity.

Musée Picasso, Antibes

The Musée Picasso at Antibes, housed in what was formerly the Château Grimaldi, is a comprehensive collection of works from one period in Picasso's career. Nearly all the paintings, drawings, sculpture, and ceramics were executed in 1946 between July and late November, during Picasso's stay there. All these works are infused with the spirit of the place—each one either captures the antique heritage of the city or represents the daily life and everyday objects associated with a thriving Mediterranean port.

In July of 1946, Jules Dor de la Souchère, curator of what was then called the Musée d'Antibes, offered Picasso space to paint at the museum. The museum had been established in 1928, and the collection was noted for its series of documents relating to Napoleon. Due to limited funds, the museum had been unable to build up a substantial selection of works of art. Many of the second-floor galleries were completely empty. Since Picasso had expressed a desire to work on a large scale, this space was ideally suited to his ambition. Materials such as plywood and fibro-cement were gathered; canvas was still scarce and difficult to obtain so soon after the war. Picasso set to work in the palace, a four-teenth-century edifice set high on a cliff overlooking the sea. It was a time of great happiness for Picasso; he was secure in his new relationship with Françoise Gilot; he had high hopes for the Communist Party, which he had just joined; and a retrospective exhibition of his work was being mount-ed at the Museum of Modern Art in New York, organized by Alfred Barr. All of these events contributed to his re-newed pleasure in life; it was an attitude he transferred to his paintings.

At Antibes, Picasso was able to create monumental works. Large-scale paintings and drawings were based on compositions and styles from his fifty years of activity. Un-expectedly called to Paris at the end of November by the death of a friend, he left all of these works at the Musée d'Antibes. First lent and finally given to the museum (which was then renamed the Musée Picasso), the works are exhib-ited in ten rooms decorated with medieval and Renaissance furniture, and some antique sculpture. Picasso later donated further drawings and ceramics to the collection.

The Musée Picasso is unique in that it displays the works of art in the very setting in which they were created. As one walks through the galleries, one can sense the plea-sure Picasso must have felt while working here. The muse-um policy has been to allow no works to leave the collection, thus maintaining the integrity of this one period of intense activity. No work has left its original setting, and as Picasso said to Dor de la Souchère: "While I'm here I'm not just going to paint some pictures. I'm going to decorate your museum for you."

Musée National Fernand Léger, Biot

The Musée Fernand Léger was founded at Biot after the death of the artist in 1953. Léger's association with Biot began in 1949, when he opened a ceramic studio there. His protégée, Nadia, was his assistant in the studio; she became his wife in 1953. Following Léger's death, Mme Léger de-veloped the vast inheritance of works of art she had received from her husband into a public museum, supplying all the funds for its organization and construction. This inheritance included drawings, sculpture, paintings, ceramics, and stud-ies for works of art on a vast scale. The museum was inau-

Musée National Fernand Léger

gurated in May 1960. The original honorary board included Pablo Picasso, Georges Braque, and Marc Chagall. In Oc-tober 1967, the Musée Fernand Léger—the land, the build-ing and the 348 works in the collection—was donated to France, and thereby became a national museum, adminis-tered by the Musées Nationaux.

The building was designed by André Svetchine in a modern, functionalist style. Construction began in 1957. The architecture incorporated several major works by Léger and the building as a whole is expressive of Léger's bold and reductivist aesthetic. The facade is dominated by one of Lé-ger's vast mural compositions; it is made of mosaic and was originally intended to be installed in the Municipal Stadium in Hanover, Germany. Measuring nearly 500 meters square, the surface is animated by the contrast between the extraor-dinary range of enamels and the black and white ceramic. The vibrant sunlight of the Midi heightens the brilliance of the mosaic; the facade itself becomes a work of art as it looms over the countryside. The interior of the museum consists of a raised first floor with a vast entrance hall illu-minated by a large stained-glass window, measuring fifty meters square, also designed by Léger. The organization and installation of these works, as well as the rest of the mu-seum's collection, was undertaken by Georges Bauquier, who also donated many pieces to the collection. Two galler-ies and one large exhibition hall serve to present drawings, gouaches, ceramics, and paintings from the years 1904 to 1955, allowing the viewer a full appreciation of Léger's unique contribution to modern art. Outside, a large terrace leads to the monumental sculpture *The Children's Garden*, a permanent installation.

A "cathedral of modern art" that takes its place

among the artistic jewels of the Côte d'Azur, this museum reveals the power of an art rich in colors—the expression of joy, light, and optimism of a creator who wanted to be an "impassioned witness to his time." As the artist said: "If destiny has borne you creative and free, with all that this word signifies in strength, expressiveness of spirit, and ruggedness, then you will live an epic life, the most beautiful but the most dangerous of all." With its broad range of works, the Musée Fernand Léger preserves and commemorates the epic life of a unique artist.

Fondation Maeght, St.-Paul de Vence

The Fondation Maeght in St.-Paul de Vence, inaugurated in 1964, is a comprehensive museum. Not only does it house an exceptional collection of modern painting and sculpture, it also sponsors concerts, dance and theater events, various workshops for visiting artists, and an experimental film studio. The aim of this foundation has been best summarized by its patron and president, Aimé Maeght: "I'd like to have people here to hammer out the new thing, whatever it is, in all the arts."

Aimé Maeght is one of the most notable art collectors of this century. He began his career in the arts as a commercial lithographer; through this profession he met Pierre Bonnard, among other artists. After the end of the Second World War he opened a gallery in Paris. His first exhibition there was of the most recent works by Matisse. Over the next few years he developed a policy that continues to characterize his gallery: to show the contemporary work of established masters and at the same time the new work of younger, unknown artists.

The Fondation Maeght is the greatest enterprise sponsored by Maeght, who has also been a publisher of magazines, art books, and lithographs. The project was initiated in the early 1950s when he and his wife Marguerite chose to restore an ancient chapel in St.-Paul in memory of their son Bernard. Gradually the project broadened to include a museum of contemporary art, gardens, and works commissioned to become a part of a large architectural complex.

After seeing Miró's studio in Palma de Mallorca, Maeght selected his architect, José Luis Sert, to build the Fondation. Sert had designed Miró's studio as a simple, clearly defined space filled with diffused sunlight. He applied similar principles to the foundation. It is comprised of a series of galleries, a residence and studio for artists, a large sculpture court, a variety of facilities to promote the arts, and the restored chapel, decorated by Braque and Ubac.

The complex has been carefully sited in a natural setting of pine trees and terraces. The buildings do not dominate the landscape; rather, they have been integrated harmoniously into the sloping terrain. To avoid monotony, the galleries are placed at different levels, and many open onto gardens. Throughout, Sert has established a rhythm of internal and external spaces: interior galleries alternate with exterior courts. The visitor is never isolated from the surrounding landscape; one can appreciate art within the museum or by wandering around the sculpture-filled gardens that encircle it.

Many of the works in the Fondation were created by artists in direct association with the initial building of the structure. These artists created decorative and monumental works that have been integrated with the building and its immediate environment. The most elaborate collaborative work in the ensemble is the *Labyrinth*, a sculpture garden that is the result of the combined efforts of Sert, Miró, and Artigas. Sert has described this collaboration: "The walls conform to the sculpture, and the sculpture to the walls and the spaces they define. They grew together as a joint work." Similarly, Giacometti oversaw the design of the Giacometti courtyard, placing his works there himself. Large mosaic walls were contributed by Chagall, Tal-Coat, Braque, and later Miró. The museum continues to be enriched by new works, and many of the recent acquisitions have also been installed by the artists themselves, as was the 1978 *Fountain* by Bury.

Each year, the Fondation Maeght organizes several exhibitions which are international in character. In addition, it sponsors and organizes many travelling exhibitions in France and other countries. The spectacular landscape of St.-Paul de Vence is as much a feature of the museum as are its works. Looking back at his creation, Maeght commented: "I don't like museums that are closed boxes. A museum should not be shut off from life. What I wanted to make here is a museum that people can step in and out of without being conscious, each time, of a change of climate. I don't want them to feel *directed*. [I want to] reinstate the individual as the measure of all things." It is this quality of individualism that makes the Fondation Maeght a special center of the arts and a unique experience for everyone who visits it.

Musée National Message Biblique
Marc Chagall, Nice

Of all the French museums on the Mediterranean this is one of the most original. In order to understand its *raison d'être*, it is necessary to understand the genesis of Marc Chagall's work here, his monumental *Message Biblique*. It constitutes a cycle of seventeen large works given to the French State in 1966 and offered to the general public on July 7, 1973, the date of the opening of the museum, on the occasion of the artist's eighty-sixth birthday.

The primary virtue of this museum is that it presents a part of Chagall's oeuvre that both echoes his deepest cultural history and reflects his most personal imaginary world. Chagall was born in the Jewish ghetto of Vitebsk, Russia. His childhood was marked by Hebraic mysticism and Jewish traditions; thus the heart of the Bible was incarnated into his everyday life. The works of the museum were chosen by him not only for their quality, but also for their significance in the history of his life as a painter. Chagall was sixty-seven when he began the *Message Biblique*. The sum of his art, poetry, and experience as a man and as an artist, this cycle is the moving witness of his desire to commemorate what he has taken from and understood about life.

In 1930 the French publisher Ambroise Vollard proposed to Chagall that he illustrate the Bible, and offered to finance a trip to Palestine. After so many years of dreaming of the Promised Land, the painter was able to tread on the soil of Israel, see the place of miracles, the sojourn of the Prophets, the wall of the Temple. The spiritual shock was strong, but Chagall responded as a painter. The light affected him profoundly—neither in his native Vitebsk nor in Paris was it so pure, so bright. While still under the influence of this inner revelation, it was this light, both physical and spiritual, that he wanted to capture in the gouaches painted in Paris on his return.

He interpreted the *Message Biblique* both poetically and epically. The gouaches that Chagall managed to preserve through the war years served as preparatory works for the large paintings which he did in Vence after 1954. He did more than 200 additional sketches before he began the seventeen great paintings from Genesis, Exodus, and The Song of Songs.

Thus, gouaches, sketches, and large paintings together form a coherent group and mark the chronology of a creation that spanned more than thirty years. It is a rare privilege to be able to follow the complete progression of so monumental a project here in this one museum. André Malraux and the architect André Hermant have offered the artist a building in which the rooms are connected to present the various works as a group. To complete this scheme, Chagall did *The Creation*, three stained-glass windows placed in the concert hall of the museum. There the creation of the world becomes a metaphor for the creative act of the artist.

The construction of the museum gave the artist the opportunity to do new things. Along with the windows he added a large mosaic (715 x 57 cm.), where images of the zodiac and the Prophet Elijah express the two visions of the destiny of man. A tapestry and sculptures complete the group, bearing witness to the relentless effort of this artist.

It is important to note that the *Message Biblique* is not limited to a purely Hebraic interpretation, for Christ figures often appear, symbolically tied to the universal message suggested by the Scriptures and made to fit Chagall's own interpretation of that message. Chagall therefore does not address himself to the person faithful to one religion or another, or the person of one political or philosophical system or another. He doesn't want to convert or win over. He wants his audience to be dazzled in front of the beauty of creation, and to be frightened as he is before the forces of destruction which threaten humankind and the world.

To further the all-encompassing preoccupations of Chagall, the museum sponsors special exhibitions. These consist of works from the ancient past to the present which celebrate the great moments of creation, sacred to the conscience of man and his idea of heaven. Musical performances are also presented in the museum. Programs in the auditorium partly reflect Chagall's taste, from his passion for Mozart and Schubert to his interest in contemporary music.

However, it is the public which is at the center of this establishment. Chagall, a man of culture and experience, wanted this museum to serve to awaken reflection in each of us. Thanks to funds put at the museum's disposal by a very active association of friends, conferences are organized on themes related to the exhibited works, guided tours are available every day free of charge, films are shown on Chagall and his work. Here, then, is a museum that is meaningful to our modern preoccupations. It is open to all cultures to show their most elevated aspects, and thus offers by poetic means a prospect of peace to the world to come.

Musée Matisse, Nice

The Musée Matisse, which stands on the hill of Cimiez, site of the ancient Cemenelum (1st-3rd century A.D.), has the advantage of presenting a collection of Henri Matisse's works in a setting he knew and loved. After 1938, the artist made Cimiez his home. Many photographs show him working in his studio in a huge Victorian building, the Hotel Regina, next to the present museum.

Matisse died in Cimiez, and after his death in 1954 his wife, Amélie Parayre, decided to create a museum in his memory. She made a substantial public donation to the city of works by the artist, thus enabling it to establish a museum devoted to Matisse. Mme Matisse also included in her gift two works by associates of the artist during the decisive period between 1900 and 1905: Albert Marquet, a lifelong friend, who painted a portrait of Mme Matisse, and André Derain, who sketched in a few vivid Fauve strokes a *Portrait of Matisse Painting*.

From among the buildings that were proposed to house the collection, Mme Matisse chose the Villa des Arènes, then called the Villa Garin or the Propriété de Gu-

Musée Matisse

bernatis, in memory of its previous owners. This building's history dates back to 1685, when the original structure was enlarged and redecorated by Jean de Gubernatis, chairman of the Senate of Nice and Ambassador of the Dukes of Savoy. It was built in the style of seventeenth-century Genoese villas, with a simple facade and trompe-l'oeil decorations. Since then, there have been no major alterations in the design.

The artist's children, Mme Georges Duthuit, Jean Matisse, and Pierre Matisse, continued to develop the museum after their mother's death, complementing her original bequest with a donation in their own names. In 1961, the entire collection was installed on the second floor of the Villa des Arènes.

The museum opened to the public in 1963; it is a studied journey through Matisse's art. From his first painting in 1890 (*Still Life with Books*), which he dared not even sign, to the brilliant Vence *Interiors* of 1947, approximately thirty oil paintings and sketches trace the evolution of his art, culminating in the colorful explosions of the late gouache cutouts. His graphic art is represented in its extraordinary variety by eighty-five independent drawings, which employ all techniques—charcoal, pencil, and pen—and by the preparatory studies for two important milestone works in Matisse's oeuvre: *The Dance* (1931–33) and the decorations for the Dominican Chapel in Vence (1948–51). Matisse's engravings are also richly represented here, as are his ceramics.

Marie Matisse, the wife of Matisse's son Jean, recently donated a collection of fifty of Matisse's sculptures, known as the Jean Matisse Donation, which represents almost the whole of the artist's sculpted work. The donation was officially placed in trust and presented to the public in 1979, at the Musée Matisse. Matisse's sculpture thus takes an important place in the museum, making Cimiez one of the few places where one can find original casts of almost all of the artist's sculpture on permanent exhibition.

A Beauvais tapestry, *Polynesia—The Sea*, brings out an aspect of Matisse's art that dominates the museum's collection. In this tapestry, the artist transposes a spiritual dream world into the concrete reality of craft.

In 1908 Matisse defined one of the aims of his art: "What I dream of is an art of balance, of purity and serenity . . . an art which might be for every mental worker, be he businessman or writer, like an appeasing influence." Through the combined efforts and generosity of this artist's family, the Musée Matisse preserves the tranquillity and balance distilled by Henry Matisse in all his art.

Musée des Beaux-Arts Jules Chéret, Nice

As the successor to the first fine arts museum of Nice, which had been founded just after the accession of Nice to France in 1860, the Musée des Beaux-Arts Jules Chéret articulates two complementary facets of the French artistic heritage: the architecture of the nineteenth century and its paintings. The collection is housed in a splendid building, a former palace, begun in 1878 by the Russian Princess Kotschoubey and finished by an American, James Thompson; its style is inspired by Genoese Mannerist architecture. After it was purchased by the city of Nice, the interior of the building was remodelled to accommodate the municipal art collections, and the museum was inaugurated on January 7, 1928. The noted Symbolist painter, Gustav-Adolf Mossa was the curator, having succeeded his father, Alexis Mossa.

The collection was assembled from important individual gifts and from treasures that had belonged to the French government since the Second Empire. Among these were works by Fragonard, Hubert Robert, and Vanloo, as well as numerous academic paintings, and Impressionist works from the Musée du Jeu de Paume. These gifts and bequests, however, do not tell the whole story: the museum's collection has grown through significant donations by generous private patrons. Baron Joseph Vitta and Maurice Fenaille, founders of the museum, gave to it what now constitutes the most complete collection in the world of the work of Jules Chéret—the creator of the modern poster—thus giving the museum its current name. Other notable donations have been made by artists and their families.

A work by Ziem was donated by his widow. Mme Bashkirtseff generously gave the museum works by her daughter Marie. Mme Clément-Carpeaux, the daughter of the sculptor, made several gifts of her father's works. Thirteen ceramics by Picasso were donated jointly by the artist and M and Mme Ramié, proprietors of the Société Madoura and the Société des Amis des Musées de Nice. Mme Dufy, the Niçoise wife of the painter, made a rich gift to the museum and later supplemented it with a magnificent bequest, creating a veritable Dufy Museum within the Chéret. This was later enriched by a consignment of Dufy works from the Réunion des Musées Nationaux. The Mossa family has given the museum over a thousand works by Alexis and Gustav-Adolf Mossa. Four canvases by Léopold Survage were given by his widow, and works of Chagall, Dufy, and Marie Laurencin were bequeathed by M Kahn. Further acquisitions were made by the city of Nice with the aid of the government and by the Société des Amis des Musées de Nice.

Aside from these donations, the Chéret Museum has for decades housed works by a number of important masters of the Second Empire and the *Belle Epoque*. Without question the portrait has predominated in the collection; however, the museum also includes many other nineteenth-century genres: history-paintings, interior scenes, still lifes, and landscapes. The Musée des Beaux-Arts Jules Chéret presents, among the museums of the Côte d'Azur, one of the most complete collections of European masters of the nineteenth century, from the Neoclassicism of the school of David to the first fires of Impressionism. The historic Kotschoubey palace is thus the nostalgic witness to the retrospective charms of an incomparable collection whose contents admirably reflect the spirit of a century.

Musée du Palais Carnolès, Menton

In 1717, Prince Antoine I of Monaco purchased the magnificent coastal site of what is now the Musée du Palais Carnolès from the Monastery of Lerins in Menton, which had owned the property since the eleventh century. It was he who built the palace, which served him as a summer residence, and designed it as a two-story building in the spirit of the Grand Trianon at Versailles, with a central section flanked by two lateral wings. The architects were Cotte, the director of the Paris Academy of Architecture, and Gabriel. The various salons were sumptuously decorated with paintings. The beautiful terraced gardens, trees, and promenades around the building were designed by Antoine Latour.

During the Revolution of 1789, the Palais Carnolès was appropriated by the state. The property then passed through many hands by sale and succession—it was a casino for several years in the 1860s—and was finally acquired in 1896 by an American, Dr. Edward P. Allis, who renovated it and made it into his private residence. He lived there until his death in Monaco in 1947. Although he made some extensive alterations and had the interior decorations restored, the building retained the architectural spirit of the des Alpes-Maritimes. The building was admitted to the Ineighteenth century, and since then no further modification has been made.

The palace was bought in 1961 by the Département ventory of Historic Monuments in 1969, and that same year the city of Menton and the Préfecture des Alpes-Maritimes agreed to convert it into a museum. After extensive reconstruction, the Musée du Palais Carnolès was inaugurated in 1977, thus becoming the thirty-third museum of the Côte d'Azur.

The core of this museum is the collection of an Englishman named Wakefield-Mori, who bequeathed his holdings of Old Master and modern paintings to the city of Menton in 1958. The paintings were catalogued, organized, and placed in a setting that reconstructed the ambience of a turn-of-the-century residence of a collector. In conjunction with this installation, all the interior decoration still in existence was once again repaired. Everything necessary was done to recreate the atmosphere of a princely mansion.

The collection that Wakefield-Mori assembled in his lifetime is richly varied; it reflects the highly personal taste of an art lover of the beginning of this century. While it includes many Italian paintings from the fourteenth to sixteenth centuries, the Flemish and Dutch schools are also well represented. Unfortunately, there are few works from the eighteenth and nineteenth centuries; however, there is a sizable body of modern art. The collection is arranged chronologically throughout the museum.

While the permanent collection of the museum is important, it is further enhanced by biennial exhibitions, which concentrate on a particular artistic theme or school. Recent contributions to the collection have been made by artists who have become honorary citizens of the city, and by artists celebrated in these biennals, such as Graham Sutherland, Kostia Terechkovitch, and Paul Delvaux. Work on the Palais Carnolès is not yet finished; three galleries have yet to be completed, and the print collection has yet to be installed. Exhibitions of modern sculpture, using the grounds for large works, also have been planned.

This most recent addition to the museums of the Côte d'Azur, now entering its fourth year of public activity, links the past with the present. The palace, once the summer retreat of the princes of Monaco, is now the home of the fine art of the city of Menton. There, a visitor can see treasures from the Early Renaissance to the vital and exciting art of today.

Plate List

Musée de l'Annonciade, St.-Tropez

GEORGES SEURAT

b. Paris, 1859
d. Paris, 1891

Study for "Canal at Gravelines"

1890
Oil on wood
15 x 25 cm. ($5^7/_8$ x $9^7/_8$ in.)

This study, from the last summer of Seurat's life, is the oldest painting in the collection. It had belonged to Signac, whose friend Georges Grammont bequeathed it to the museum.

Seurat conducted rigorous formal studies in advance of each painting. He isolated the details of the composition and the elements of the spectrum in sketches like this one. He then worked out a synthesis of the studies to produce paintings of consummate clarity.

Each summer he left his studio to return to the waterside which so often was the central subject of his work. In his last summer, at Gravelines, he made four small paintings of the canal, and eight studies. The final paintings are masterpieces of serenity. Nothing disrupts the stillness of the scene; every aspect of the composition contributes to the eternal quiet. The reduced range of color values allowed him to concentrate on delicate tonal shifts, revealing the poetic arrangements of line and form that had begun to interest him after the establishment of his color theory. Light is diffused, and the masses are proportionally related through a perfectly harmonious geometry. Seurat had become concerned with the framing of the composition; he painted a narrow dark band to contain the sketch. The touches of pigment are complex in themselves as well as in their juxtapositions. There are dots within dots, several hues in many of the seemingly single touches of the brush. The simple study is in fact composed of complex units of tone.

The Divisionist technique of color painting was developed in collaboration with artists who shared Seurat's desire to integrate the discoveries of optical science with the activity of painting. The movement toward a theoretical synthesis of all human activity defined the intellectual environment of the late nineteenth century, and Seurat was as much an intellectual as he was an artist. That there would be fixed laws of color relationships and linear arrangements he took as given; the discovery of these laws occupied his mind. He took as his task the invention of painting techniques drawn not from the appearance of nature but from its underlying rules of proportion and contrast.

At his death at the age of thirty-one, Seurat left some 700 sketches, drawings, and paintings. Signac, reflecting on the death of his youthful friend, wrote three years later: "He had passed the painters' problems in review and said the last word, more or less, on all of them."

16

PAUL SIGNAC

b. Paris, 1863
d. Paris, 1935

Harbor of St.-Tropez

1899
Oil on canvas
65 x 81 cm. (25⅝ x 31⅞ in.)

Paul Signac has a special place in the history of this museum. He helped to gather the nucleus of the collection and a number of its paintings were his personal donation. Through his teaching and writing, he influenced the generation of artists represented in this collection. He was a perceptive critic as well, and conducted open galleries at his studio every Monday. As vice-president and then president of the Salon des Indépendants, he knew the artists at work in Paris. As an ardent propagandist of Divisionist color theory, he sought out artists everywhere, and brought them to his St.-Tropez atelier. In his diaries, he recorded the aesthetic ideas of his time, for which we continue to be in his debt.

Divisionist color theory may be reduced to a statement of the law of contrast: a color will be seen at its most intense when it is adjacent to its complementary. The separation of color elements by means of small strokes of the brush on the canvas will lead to the optical mixture of color on the retina of the viewer; the optical mixture will be more brilliant than can be achieved by the actual mixture of pigments on the painted surface. Signac defended this technique: "I dislike all juggling or rubbing that tarnishes [the purity of the brushstroke]. Why—when one can paint with jewels—should one use muck instead? It is the love of beautiful color which makes us paint like that and not the taste for the 'dot,' as some fools pretend."

His painting of the port of St.-Tropez exemplifies the theory and shows the glowing clarity of his style. From every corner of the canvas, with each touch of the brush, he set down a clean mark and arranged the areas in complex and beautiful geometry. Each cloud and sail, every section of water and sky is a perfect model of the Divisionist ideal.

The Artificial Pond at Cézanne's House

1920
Pencil and watercolor on paper
30 x 45 cm. (11¹³⁄₁₆ x 17¾ in.)

In the watercolor reproduced here, Signac has brushed in dazzling clusters of color with so sure and free a hand that the result seems almost casual. The drawn lines are in dynamic tension with the watercolor. There are calligraphic shapes amid the long and short brushstrokes, some laden with color and others thin and shimmering. The atmosphere is transparent. His color sense is impeccable; every area of multiple hues is a miniature study of color compatibility.

The lines are deft and light, simple curves that suggest a direction or imply a form. The many abrupt verticals work against the natural emphasis of the horizon. The arabesques define trees, a rock, a statue; they give us the landscape, but our pleasure comes from the remarkable patterns of color, which Signac made bloom on the paper as if in response to the blooming of nature. He once said, "I have too often felt the yoke of nature not to dread it." This watercolor shows that he could create a counterpoint to nature, true to the craft of painting and to the human experience of beauty.

19

HENRI EDMOND CROSS

b. Douai, 1856
d. St.-Clair, 1910

The Shore at St.-Clair

1906–08
Oil on canvas
65 x 81 cm. (25⅝ x 31⅞ in.)

Henri Edmond Cross was one of the founders of the Salon des Indépendants in 1884. Cross, Seurat, and Signac met there, and formed friendships based on their shared aesthetic concerns. They had turned from the romantic hedonism of the Impressionists and sought in its place a universal science of line, decoration, and color. Cross wrote that "in creation there is, together with instinct, a great deal of willpower, and will can only derive from a precise basis. This precision occupies me. . . . My sensations, as a result of the nature of my artistic temperament, ask for a grammar, rhetoric, and logic."

Cross lived near Signac at St.-Tropez, and helped to entertain the artists who gathered at Signac's atelier. Signac, always an eager instructor, may have been less influential with some of the younger painters than Cross, whose spirit was gentler and more sympathetic. His paintings are lush and full of sinuous rhythms. He organizes his masses in long arabesques that have a kinship to Art Nouveau, but his subject is always the countryside. With little mosaic-like daubs of color he delineates the trees and rocks of the coastline, as in this painting of the rolling hills by the beach. In the image of the woman in white we see the poetic sensibility of this artist, whose search for a science of painting was, in part, a struggle against his own tendency to sentiment. Painted with only touches of blue, to suggest the shadows on her dress and hat, the woman seems dappled with light, radiant.

He was intensely concerned with the decisions one had to make when painting from nature. "One cannot put everything on a canvas," he wrote. "One can put only very little. These few things become everything—the work of the man." In his studio, working from sketches made at the site, he created a world of balanced masses, complementary curves, and "chromatic harmonies completely invented and established, so to speak, without reference to nature as a point of departure."

21

ANDRE DERAIN

b. Chatou, 1888
d. Chambourcy, 1954

Houses of Parliament

1905
Oil on canvas
81 x 100 cm. (31⅞ x 39⅜ in.)

Using the color science of Seurat and Signac, Derain composed masses of flecked color with his own concern for order amid the tempest of nature. "I see the future only in composition," he wrote in a letter to Vlaminck in 1906. Two years later he commented to a visitor that "nature gives me the material with which to construct a world of my own"—a clear statement of a central Fauve tenet. The canvas was a battlefield between the image found in nature and the image invented by the artist engaged with his material and his imagination. Eventually, Derain repudiated the experiments of his youth, and turned in his work to traditional interpretations of nature. "Fauvism," he wrote, "was our ordeal by fire."

This is one of several paintings of historic buildings on the Thames that Derain made on his first visit to London. He was an intellectual who studied every tendency in art; he knew the current ideas and here integrated them with the earlier vision of Turner. In this painting of Westminster he meticulously orchestrates the myriad marks in diagonals radiating from the sun-disc, blue and red glowing on the pale background. In the broad central band, his brushstrokes are cross-hatched in perfect balance. The surface of the building seems to shimmer, yet we feel the mass and solidity beneath the exterior. The design is organized around the tower above the horizon, the band of light through the water, and the swirl of red paint massed at the river's edge, behind which the building appears to recede into the picture plane. Derain preserved this illusion of distance within the overall flat surface design.

The poet Apollinaire claimed that Fauvism was born at the meeting of Matisse and Derain, and Cubism at the meeting of Picasso and Derain—a testament to the passion in his painting, the breadth of his knowledge, and the intensity of his personality.

MAURICE DE VLAMINCK

b. Paris, 1876
d. Rueil-la-Gadalière, 1958

Boat Wash Houses at Chatou

1905/06
Oil on canvas
54 x 73 cm. (21¼ x 28¾ in.)

The Fauves were bound by youthful friendships: Matisse and Marquet were students together, Braque and Friesz painted the same scenes, and Vlaminck and Derain shared a studio on the island of Chatou. Derain called it "a sort of 'Barbizon' at the gates of Paris." He noted that Renoir and Courbet had painted there, and wrote, "Once I saw Degas in a barque on the Seine [near Chatou], wearing a thick fur coat in the height of August." This was in a little book called *Chatou* which he and Vlaminck wrote and illustrated. Vlaminck closed the book with these words: "The color of everything that enchanted us—that was CHATOU!"

After Derain had seen Turner's river scenes in London (see page 23), he may have influenced Vlaminck, who began to paint many versions of the bridge and waterside at Chatou. Although his paintings celebrate the landscape, Vlaminck wrote in 1906 that nature was a pretext, through which "I wanted to reveal myself utterly, with all my good qualities and defects." He did not rework his paintings, choosing to let his original impressions reveal what they would of his inner state.

Vlaminck proclaimed himself to be self-taught and uninfluenced. Yet he announced in his autobiography, *Dangerous Corner*, that when he first saw the paintings of Van Gogh his "soul was overcome with joy and despair. On that day I loved Van Gogh more than I loved my own father." The Salon des Indépendants paid homage to both Van Gogh and Seurat in 1905. Vlaminck, by then in Paris, absorbed from both these painters techniques recognizable in this scene. In the sky each brushstroke is a separate surge of color, and the composition throughout is built of discrete color blocks. In all his painting of this time, primary colors were laid in directly from the tube, with little reference to their actual appearance in nature. The bridge is drawn with emphatic perpendicular marks that deny traditional perspective and stack the far planes upright on the picture surface: the small houses at the upper right seem attached to the elongated orange vertical pole rising from the house below. In all these respects—the organization of intense pure colors, the assertive brush marks, the tilted picture plane, and the transcendental use of landscape—*Boat Wash Houses at Chatou* is an exemplary Fauve painting.

24

25

EMILE OTHON FRIESZ

b. Le Havre, 1879
d. Paris, 1949

Harbor of Antwerp

1906
Oil on canvas
69 x 80 cm. (27^3/$_{16}$ x 31^1/$_2$ in.)

Like so many of the Fauves, Friesz painted along the Mediterranean coast, enchanted by the light, the geometry of ships in port, and the seaside horizon.

He said in 1904 that "color appeared as our savior." He wished "to give the equivalent of sunlight by a technique consisting in colored orchestrations—impassioned transpositions (based on natural emotion)." Friesz overlaid paint and allowed some mixing of the pigments, despite the assertion in Divisionist color theory that such mixing would dull the luminosity that was desired in the painting. The assertions were mistaken; he achieved a brilliant mother-of-pearl iridescence. He used an emphatically tilted perspective, as if the viewer were perched on a cloud above the port. Light seems to dominate the composition, radiating upward from the water. All the incident of portside is secondary to the display of light in sky and river; there is more motion and restless energy in the clouds and water than in the crowds that are busy at the water's edge.

Friesz had an extensive art education. He began his studies when quite young, took instruction with Corot, admired Delacroix, and was influenced by Monet. His comrades among the Fauves were Dufy and Braque, with whom he shared an affinity for multihued, curvilinear motifs. Each of them used the radically upturned perspective that had so intrigued French painters in the still lifes of Cézanne.

They saw themselves as radical modernists, addressing the most advanced aesthetic issues, but Friesz carried into the new century the old Impressionist desire to create an approximation of pure light, revealing the fullness of forms. The light which entranced him works here to fill out the clouds and bring to clarity the boats on the shimmering water.

GEORGES BRAQUE

b. Argenteuil, 1882
d. Paris, 1963

Village at L'Estaque

1906
Oil on canvas
60 x 73 cm. (23⅝ x 28¾ in.)

This lyrical landscape is one of the small number of paintings Braque made in the Fauve manner. In the summer of 1906 in Antwerp with Othon Friesz, he began an extensive exploration of color relationships. Friesz then encouraged him to visit L'Estaque, in the Midi, where he made the paintings that brought him his first success—uninhibited landscapes which were shown and sold at the next Salon.

This glowing painting from that autumn under the Mediterranean sun shows how ready he was for the Fauve aesthetic, which was then at its height. The luminosity of the painting derives from alignments of complementary color brushed in lightly to allow the white ground of the canvas to mediate. The variety of strokes, dots, and color masses gives the painting its sense of dancing motion. The curving lines at the edge of the clouds, trees, roadbed, and hillside sweep the composition around the stable central rectangles. These sinuous, varicolored outlines were Braque's signature device.

In three successive summers at L'Estaque he worked through the technical problems that interested the Fauves: shifting perspective, decorative organization with primary colors, and the increasingly problematic relationship between the painted surface and natural objects. By 1908 he had attenuated his palette to mostly earth tones and had begun disciplined investigations of form and structure within a strictly designed framework, his image now free of the conventional depiction of three dimensions. He was soon in daily collaboration with Picasso, and his Fauve period was over.

29

HENRI MATISSE

b. Cateau-Cambrésis, 1869
d. Cimiez, 1954

The Gypsy

1906
Oil on canvas
55 x 46 cm. (21⅝ x 18⅛ in.)

After viewing the Matisse paintings at the Salon d'Automne of 1905, the admiring critic Vauxcelles wrote that the work "would have the destiny of a Christian maiden surrendered to the wild beasts [*fauves*] of the circus," referring thus to the hostile public as the *fauves*. (He referred to the painters as *fauves* in a later paragraph in that same complimentary review.) On exhibition were the paintings Matisse had made during his summer at the St.-Tropez studio of Paul Signac, where Henri Cross was also host.

The Gypsy is a vivid example of the individual way Matisse adapted their Divisionist color theory. The adjacent splashes of red and green around the left eye, the segments of brilliant color that shape the body, and all the vibrating juxtapositions of color serve the overall pattern, while simultaneously developing a sly and witty portrait. Although Matisse made slight reference to the appearance of the model, he created a decidedly feminine image, at once soft and saucy. Other painters in the Fauve group concentrated on landscape, and used it to solve problems of color and composition rather than to interpret nature. Matisse painted still lifes, interiors, landscapes, and a striking series of portraits in which his color and compositional solutions worked also to clarify character. In this example, the space is ambivalent, the design is buoyant and assertive, and at the same time the personality dominates.

The Gypsy was one of the early Matisse paintings purchased by Leo and Gertrude Stein. She wrote of the other painters in Paris that "some were certainly wanting to be doing what this one was doing that is wanting to be one clearly expressing something." Indeed, none of them used the Fauve style with such expressive audacity.

31

HENRI MATISSE

Interior at Nice

1920
Oil on canvas
46 x 65 cm. (18$\frac{1}{8}$ x 25$\frac{5}{8}$ in.)

"Once, I wouldn't leave my paintings hanging on the wall, because they reminded me of moments when I was excited and I didn't like to see them again when I was calm. Now, I try to imbue my paintings with calm and I go over them until I have succeeded." With this statement, written in 1908, Matisse put his years of Fauve painting behind him. When we compare *The Gypsy* of 1905 (page 31) with this restrained and delicate painting, we see how far he advanced in subduing the Fauve palette, and in elaborating the pattern of his design. Here, a meticulous order of diagonals in the lower half of the painting, supporting the verticals of the upper half, and the central horizontal arm of Mlle. Matisse at rest on the table, show that Matisse could control the psychological power of geometry. We are drawn into this corner. Yet all emotional clues are blocked; the faces reveal nothing; the hands are blurred. We feel that a moment has been interrupted. Our attention moves from the personal vignette to the surrounding detail: anemones in brilliant hues, the heads of the women raised like flowers, flower patterns on the wall and blouse—all in exquisite array upon the picture plane.

In the years immediately following his Fauve experiments, Matisse had seen Islamic art at a major exhibition in Munich and also visited Moscow, Andalusia, and Morocco. "Persian miniatures," he wrote, "revealed to me all the possibilities of my senses. Because of its immense detail, this art suggests a larger space, a truly plastic space, and it helped me to go beyond intimate painting." In this painting there is a lingering sense of character, but increasingly Matisse was painting models as decorative artifacts, emblems of elegance in environments dense with orderly detail.

When Matisse established his permanent home at Nice in 1917 he painted many interiors. He showed one, without a figure, to Renoir in his only visit to the old painter. (Renoir argued with him against the use of black, which had entered his range of colors.) For the series of interiors, he arranged various objects in scenes with and without a figure, near open windows or with shutters drawn—a series of elegant statements about the decorative possibilities of the commonplace.

33

KEES VAN DONGEN

b. Delfshaven, 1877
d. Monte Carlo, 1968

The Gypsy

1911
Oil on canvas
46 x 55 cm. (18⅛ x 21⅝ in.)

In this portrait, perhaps of Fernande Olivier, Picasso's friend, Van Dongen used the garish green facial shadow that often appeared in his portraits. Here, the color suggests decay and seems a commentary on her sensuality. The face is vacuous, a ghostly circle empty of revelation of the model's character. As in so many of his portraits, her posture and dress suggest pliant sexuality. The gypsy is caught in a narrow space. She is framed by planes of red and blue, the color scraped away to set off the luminous sphere of her face, the curve of her arm, and the loose shawl and robe.

"The majority of women are painters, in their own individual fashion," Van Dongen wrote, for his models chose their own costumes and poses, usually opting for a dramatic stance and exotic garb. He developed the portraits with a minimalist drawing style in which the figure and gesture appear almost in silhouette.

Van Dongen had a long, varied career. In 1908 he showed with the German Expressionist group Die Brücke. Later he was a successful fashion illustrator for popular journals. He became a favorite in society and for most of his life painted portraits commissioned by wealthy patrons. At the time of *The Gypsy* he was living with Picasso in the Bateau Lavoir tenement in Paris. In his last years he lived in a villa in Monaco (which he dubbed *Bateau Lavoir*), among the rich and royal who had made him famous.

KEES VAN DONGEN

Women at the Balustrade

1911
Oil on canvas
81 x 100 cm. (31⅞ x 39⅜ in.)

Throughout his long career, Kees van Dongen used the pure-color palette of the Fauves; however, his character studies are more reminiscent of his seventeenth-century compatriot Frans Hals than of his Fauve contemporaries. He knew Signac and his theories, he showed with the Fauves and with the German Expressionists, and he lived with Picasso in 1906, but no painterly influence had as much impact on him as the nightlife and lowlife of Paris. Van Dongen did not join in the evolution toward freeing painting of its dependence on nature.

He is remembered as one who recorded the *Belle Epoque*, that imagined era of easy pleasure before World War I. In fact his interest was in the social periphery. He worked as a carnival roustabout and painted its clowns and belly dancers. He often painted women like this one, women whose expressions and postures suggest a lascivious invitation. He made this painting after a trip to Spain and Morocco; in the introduction to a catalogue of the paintings from that trip, he wrote: "A certain immodesty is truly a virtue, as is the absence of respect for many respectable things." In fact, his painting of a nude, in the 1913 Salon d'Automne, was removed by the police for obscenity.

Van Dongen's strong jarring color is always emblematic. Here the bright red earring, the green shadow below the lip, and ocher skin tone betoken the tantalizing. His compositional decisions are wily: although the painting is of two women, one is seen only in arcs of intense color. The elaborately patterned tapestry establishes her presence, and it frames the main figure. Broad areas of color and a simplified color range set off the pale clothing and slim torso, largely concealed by her arm and the struts of the balustrade. The face we see in full is an insolent mask, but it seems a mask of her self, not one which conceals her personality.

Van Dongen had an expressive graphic line, varied in its thickness and edge. He could suggest fleeting motion in his drawing, as he does here in the model's half-smile, the slightly forward tilt of her body, and the hand about to be offered.

36

GEORGES ROUAULT

b. Paris, 1871
d. Paris, 1958

Biblical Landscape

1935
Oil on canvas
53 x 73 cm. (20⅞ x 28¾ in.)

Rouault and Matisse were students of Gustave Moreau, in the same class at the Ecole Nationale des Beaux-Arts. Matisse and Marquet left to conduct their own studies and to learn from sources outside the academy; and indeed, it was a common story for the young Fauves to scorn formal education in art. For Rouault, however, the academy was the source and center of his artistic life. He was a grateful, adept student of Moreau, sharing with his teacher a belief that through art one may express the most deeply felt religious conviction. For both of them, art was commentary and parable.

This painting has an innocence not usually found in Rouault's work. The familiar sense of sin and doom is absent, although the urgency of his larger concerns can be intuited from the dramatic rendering of the sky. He painted color upon color, scraping away in the later stages so that earlier colors would gleam through. The wonder of his vision is that the images painted in this way are never muddy. More layers of light than we can see seem to lurk behind the painted image, as if the paint were not on canvas but on a window. The distant sun dominates the landscape, and all pictorial movement is in its direction; everything flows from the right edge toward the left, past that solar eye.

Rouault was one of the founders of the Salon d'Automne. Moreau was by then dead, and his student, in search of inspiration, developed a new awareness of Cézanne, who was honored at the Salon of 1904. He studied closely Cézanne's methods for depicting volumes in a precisely conveyed space, and he adopted Cézanne's use of cobalt ground, as in this painting. This is a remarkably beautiful, richly colored work, emotionally tranquil for so passionate an artist.

39

ARISTIDE MAILLOL

b. Banyuls-sur-Mer, 1861
d. Banyuls-sur-Mer, 1944

Woman Doing Her Hair

1919–20
Bronze
81 x 34 x 30 cm. (31⁷⁄₈ x 13³⁄₈ x
   11¹³⁄₁₆ in.)

Maillol lived all his life at his birthplace on the Spanish Mediterranean. The models for his sculptures were girls of the countryside, and in their type he saw his ideal, of which this is so lovely an example: a young woman with high pelvis, full thigh, and long, sturdy torso. He had come to sculpture when past the age of forty, already a master of weaving and dying, which had been his early career. There seems to have been no period of struggle with the new medium; his first bronzes are as persuasive as this work, as full of presence. There is no extraneous detail here. The gesture of the woman at her coiffure is subordinated to the grace of all the curves and to her assured posture. As always in his work, there is the sense of perfect stability.

Maillol's method of work was meticulous. In the drawing studio he would prepare dozens of studies. (He once told a student: "The sculptor must draw his model again and again, from all sides.") He would draw the articulation of a knee, the bend of an arm, and the inclination of the neck at every angle. Then, alone in his workshop, he would search out the form from the block, striving always for the perfectly generalized, universal image, with every aspect of the stance and gesture in balance. Always he sculpted the robust and healthy body. His was the classical ideal. Viewing an ancient, sea-worn Venus, he said: "Look there, that figure has been my teacher! ... A statue must be beautiful even when its original surface has perished and it has been worn as smooth as a pebble." His goal was eternal grace embodied in architectonic sculpture, to be seen in the round, unambiguous in its idealization of the naked body.

41

PIERRE BONNARD

b. Fontenay-aux-Roses, 1867
d. Le Cannet, 1947

Nude Before the Fireplace

1917
Oil on canvas
77 x 60 cm. ($30^5/_{16}$ x $23^5/_8$ in.)

What is most striking in this painting is its sumptuous color. The forms take shape in a pool of color, with just enough clarity of definition—and no more—to convince us of the painter's concern with the figure. The power of the painting is in the marbling of essentially unharmonious tones. The equilibrium Bonnard maintains between color concentration and the reference to visual reality characterizes his work. Although his career spanned six decades, through violent changes in the concept of visual art, he always used his color-saturated style to serve an essentially conservative pattern of forms.

Bonnard worked very slowly, often taking years to complete a canvas, and yet often he managed to preserve the initial impression, the quick, unconscious gesture. Everything in the arrangement of the picture—the cropped edge, revealing mirror, and simplified geometry—brings us closer to the woman than the painter could have been. The woman is isolated, not only in her boudoir but in the frame. Only a few suggestions of a world beyond the canvas exist, emerging from and dividing the areas of elaborate color variations, like the sheen on a collection of deep-sea shells.

EDOUARD VUILLARD

b. Cuiseaux, 1868
d. La Baule, 1940

Two Women Under the Lamp

1892
Oil on canvas
33 x 41 cm. (13 x 16⅛ in.)

Vuillard often placed the figures of his interiors in a corner or near adjacent doors. The perpendiculars of his interior architecture encase the figures in a stable structure. Strong horizontals and verticals move in from the edge of the canvas to fix our attention on the figures and the light at play around them. This method was met with derision early in his career; the public is said to have turned the paintings upside down, perhaps in scorn of the prominence of these assertive perpendiculars.

Here, the most complex decoration is concentrated between the dark forms of the women, in the intense hue of the lamp, the splash of bright yellow to its left, and the arrangement of forms around the hand at rest by its base. Our view of all that is revealed in the light of the lamp is conditioned by the dark surrounding masses and the radically tilted perspective. In the confluence of light and figures at the intimate center of the painting, Vuillard affirms the contentments of domesticity. His friend Mallarmé wrote of the "healing quiet of the hearth," to which all of Vuillard's work bears witness.

The Soup

1900–01
Oil on cardboard
35 x 61 cm. (13¾ x 24 in.)

Edouard Vuillard was a contemporary of Matisse. They were both concerned with the representation of interiors, with women at home, and with the decorative pattern of homely objects (see page 33); however, they had very different attitudes toward these motifs. Daily tasks do not cease under Vuillard's observing eye. He records the ongoing activities of the house, and concentrates our attention upon the patterns created by human interaction. In this painting, the most emphatic design is established in the triangle between the woman's lap and the face of the child; the rest of the painting is organized in long rectangles expanding away from the figures. As always in his paintings, Vuillard maintains a reticent propriety: the figures are engaged with each other, and he does not alter the perspective to reveal their emotion.

Some years after his theater friend Lugné-Poé shared a studio with Vuillard (and Bonnard and Maurice Denis), he wrote of Vuillard that "he was unaffectedly good." We do not need a general theory about the relationship between an artist's character and the quality of his work to agree that, in this case, the statement of character could be inferred from the painting. Vuillard befriended Renoir in his late years and, like Renoir, declared the primacy of domestic happiness to be the source of beauty.

44

ALBERT MARQUET

b. Bordeaux, 1875
d. Paris, 1947

Harbor at Sète

1920
Oil on canvas
65 x 81 cm. (25⅝ x 31⅞ in.)

The Fauve movement with which Marquet was identified was, to a large extent, a coincidence of youthful friendships coupled with the interest in pure color which was characteristic of European paintings at the turn of the century. For a few years, this congruence of personal friendships and contemporary concerns produced some paintings of brilliant luminosity. The same painters later pursued separate, more formal goals, as their common early concern for the precedence of color over texture, line, and structure subsided.

Marquet, one of the founders of the Salon d'Automne in 1903, and always at the center of the Fauve fellowship, employed in his later work a restrained palette and a close observation of nature. He had studied with Cross and Signac at St.-Tropez, and he knew how to use their pure colors and technique (see pages 21 and 19). His natural concerns, however, produced more dignified and traditional paintings. This painting, for example, suggests contemplation, rather than a world in motion or a revolution in art. For the controlled elegance of his work, Matisse compared him to Hokusai.

Marquet travelled widely and painted the ports of Europe. He visited Tunis, Algiers, Marseilles, and Naples. Even at home in Paris he lived at the water's edge, on the Seine near the Ile St.-Louis. He loved delicate nuance in color, and illusionist perspective. There are signs of his lively drawing style in the little free-form figures that appear here on the bridge and docks. He made quick sketches everywhere he went, with a flowing line that crisscrossed the page as if he could not stop the pencil, so rapidly did he record the passing scene.

47

RAOUL DUFY

b. Le Havre, 1877
d. Forcalquier, 1953

Racetrack at Deauville

1928
Oil on canvas
54 x 65 cm. (21¼ x 25⅝ in.)

This is the first of six paintings by Dufy of the racetrack at Deauville. The last of the series was completed over twenty years later. (There are other paintings of the race itself.) He had begun painting horses and racetracks in 1923, and returned to these subjects throughout his life. The constant activity at the track suited him, for he had become fascinated with the attempt to capture rapid motion on the stable picture plane. He wrote of this in his notebook: "What one should remember is that a line describes more especially movement than a form. A silhouette is a movement and not a form."

All that characterizes his work is evident here: the scene presented in strictly frontal view, the near and far planes stacked in horizontal bands upon the canvas, and atmospheric clarity—it is always fair weather in Dufy's world. However, the interplay between the jaunty squiggle of his drawn line and his flamboyant color is the most delightful aspect of his painting. Forms and figures appear through jabs of red or white or mixed pigments; the whole pattern of color is a reconfirmation and reminder of his enthusiastic career among the Fauves.

Dufy was a tireless worker. He designed fabrics and tapestries, municipal murals, theater decor, and even the swimming pool for the ocean liner *Normandie*. Again and again he returned to the same themes and locations, making dozens of drawings and studies for his paintings of racecourses and regattas, homages to Bach and Mozart, seas and circuses. This concentration on a set of themes was for him a kind of laboratory research, performed on scenes which he felt would reveal their most artful configurations only upon constant scrutiny. "The artist works for himself," he wrote. "It is his greatest joy to bring images hitherto confused into the light of day." Dufy's contribution was to wed a personal, unique style of drawing with the dashing color sense he developed in his youth.

ROGER DE LA FRESNAYE

b. Le Mans, 1885
d. Grasse, 1925

The Rower

1914
Oil on canvas
60 x 80 cm. (23⅝ x 31½ in.)

The Rower is an unfinished oil painting, but a drawing of the same subject also exists, as well as a lithograph dated the same year. As the shifting planes suggest, La Fresnaye was moving toward a complete identification with Cubism. During the years before the First World War, he accelerated the dissolution of figure into background, using the Cubist analysis of form to achieve an increasingly decorative structure.

No clear feature identifies the rower. La Fresnaye was an avid oarsman, so this painting could be taken as a form of self-portraiture. Later, after being wounded in the war (he was eventually to die from those wounds), he painted his own face over and over on images of a man with large, strong hands, whose body was shrunken, debilitated.

MARCEL GROMAIRE

b. Noyelles-sur-Sambre, 1892
d. Paris, 1971

The Wash

1930
Oil on wood
41 x 33 cm. (16⅛ x 13 in.)

Marcel Gromaire, fascinated with the human form, gave the monumentality of sculpture to his painted figures of women at their daily tasks. His was an art of social commentary. He painted soldiers, workers, a modern pietà as if they were universal symbols, using an attenuated Cubist style. His palette was always simple: a few broad areas of translucent colors arranged on Divisionist principles.

After the Second World War, pattern asserted itself over the issues of his earlier work. Blazing sunlight broke up the integrity of his forms and penetrated into deeper spaces of forests and cityscapes. In the paintings of the 1930s, however, he concentrated on the figure. This tableau appears in a proscenium-like space; the momentary action is preserved as a theatrical spectacle, for, as he wrote, "art is the mirror of things that are lasting."

Musée Picasso, Antibes

PABLO PICASSO

b. Malaga, 1881
d. Mougins, 1973

Head of a Woman with Chignon

1933
Cement
146 cm. high (57½ in.)

Though most noted for his activity as a painter, Picasso created a number of important sculptures throughout his career. Between 1929 and 1934, an intense period of productivity yielded a group of three-dimensional pieces, mostly done in plaster and clay, but also carried out in metal. A series of four monumental female heads were executed in bronze in 1932 at Picasso's studio at Boisgeloup. Two of these four were copied in cement in 1933 and in 1935 and presented in the Spanish Pavilion of the International Exhibition in Barcelona. They are now included in the Picasso Museum.

In 1932, Picasso was living with his new mistress, Marie-Thérèse Walter, whom he had met near the end of 1931. A blond, sensual beauty, Marie-Thérèse inspired a series of etchings of colossal heads, as well as their sculptural counterparts, the four bronze heads of Boisgeloup.

The *Head of a Woman with Chignon* takes the finely chiselled Roman profile of Marie-Thérèse and exaggerates it for an intensely plastic effect. The large nose, bundle of hair, triangular head, and long neck are assembled into a composition of elegant forms. The clarity and simplicity of the piece are comparable to the Hellenic sculpture of ancient Greece, which was certainly well known to Picasso from his many visits to the Louvre. The "classical" spirit of the sculpture heralds Picasso's *Antipolis* paintings, executed in the autumn of 1946 at Antibes, with their evocations of myth and the ancient world.

53

PABLO PICASSO

The Goat

1946
Oil on fibro-cement
120 x 150 cm. (47¼ x 59¹⁄₁₆ in.)

In 1946, Picasso was offered the opportunity to work at the Grimaldi Palace (now the Picasso Museum in Antibes) with enough space to compose paintings of monumental size. Except for isolated cases, such as *Guernica* of 1937, Picasso had not previously worked on such a large scale. In July, he, along with his mistress Françoise Gilot, moved into the palace, a fourteenth-century castle set on the edge of the Mediterranean. This period was a happy one for Picasso: 1946 brought the first summer of peace Europe had seen in ten years, and his new membership in the French Communist Party filled him with hope for the future. These factors contributed to the idyll of happiness that pervades his paintings from this season at Antibes. Picasso, moved by the sense of antiquity he experienced at Antibes, proceeded to paint scenes inspired by classical mythology and pastoral literature. He was also fascinated by the people and objects around him; the local animals and sea creatures particularly caught his fancy.

This drawing of a goat reflects the lyricism of the *Antipolis* paintings (see pages 57, 59). The stoic peacefulness of the animal's expression is a depiction of Picasso's own inner calm. The goat would again be used as a symbol in the 1950s when Picasso sculpted his image of hope, a *Pregnant She-Goat*. The goat reproduced here is composed of a series of graphic and regular lines that sweep along the concave back to the sharp, angular plane of the creature's flank. The front half is modelled with smudges of shading, while the back half remains linear, minimally describing the shape of the body, particularly the conical, two-pronged hoofs. This contrast of forms is essentially a play between three-dimensionality and abstract two-dimensionality in this simple, yet poignantly beautiful work.

PABLO PICASSO

Joie de Vivre (Pastorale)

1946
Oil on fibro-cement
120 x 250 cm. (47¼ x 98⁷⁄₁₆ in.)

The monumental *Joie de Vivre* translates, in painted form, Picasso's intense happiness during the Antibes period of 1946. The work is imbued with the pagan spirit of a bacchanalia, with figures dancing, leaping, and making music. In a friezelike, horizontal arrangement reminiscent of classical painting and sculpture, a centaur plays a flute, a full-breasted Maenad dances, two fauns leap about, and a seated satyr plays a panpipe. A yellow, white, and grey boat sails at the top left, interjecting an element of the local life of the fishing village. The screaming menace of *Guernica* (1937) is forgotten and is replaced here by smiling faces in a lighthearted composition with pure, clear colors.

The mythological subject was partly inspired by Antibes itself, which was the site of a port in antiquity. Picasso remarked of Antibes that "this antiquity seizes hold of me every time." And on the back of *Joie de Vivre* he wrote "Antipolis," the ancient Roman name of the town. The production of paintings, drawings, and sculpture is his evocation of a primeval, pagan freedom, a freedom which is evident in *Joie de Vivre*. The influence of antiquity was not a new element in Picasso's art: in 1923 he had sketched centaurs and mythological creatures. However, the thematic and stylistic sources for *Joie de Vivre* dated from 1944. During that August, while fighting was taking place in the streets of Paris, Picasso spent six days feverishly copying, in watercolor, Poussin's *Triumph of Pan* in the Louvre. This seventeenth-century bacchic scene of satyrs, goats, and children later provided material for the Antibes paintings.

Picasso must also have been inspired by Matisse's 1907 interpretation of the subject, with its unleashed, wild dance. Picasso's *Joie de Vivre* succeeds magnificently in transferring the spirit of a past age to the modern one.

56

57

PABLO PICASSO

Triptych: Satyr, Faun, and Centaur

1946
Oil and ripolin enamel on fibro-
  cement
250 x 360 cm. (98⁷⁄₁₆ x 141¾ in.)

Another painting in the *Antipolis* series, which reflects Picasso's fascination with antiquity, is this enormous triptych of a satyr, faun, and centaur, each represented in a separate panel. The work is essentially a monumental "altarpiece" to Picasso's happiness of 1946. A cat-faced satyr sits cross-legged, absorbed in playing a flute; it is a scene reminiscent of the blissful, flute-playing shepherds of ancient Greek idylls. A faun capers merrily in the central panel, leaping high above the earth (indicated by a summarily drawn line). On the right, a solidly built centaur carries a trident, smiling gleefully.

The three representations, in oil and enamel on fibro-cement, are sketched in decisive black strokes on a white ground. The contrast between black and white, and the emphasis on the linear element recall ancient Greek vase painting. This antique influence is also evident in the rendition of the figures. For example, Picasso painted the torso of the centaur full front, yet the horse portion is seen in profile. Picasso's lack of regard for "correct" appearances is taken further with the whimsical treatment of the satyr, whose tail has been brought around to his left side. The faun is almost simplistic in form; a series of angular lines describe the bent legs and the sharp, two-pronged hoofs. Counterbalancing these irregularities, the lopsided, grinning face of the faun, like the bewhiskered visage of the centaur, is entirely captivating.

Beneath the crisp, angular lines of this masculine, bacchic theme, is a sense of carefree, sensual pleasure derived from ancient pastoral scenes, whose essence was the basis of Picasso's world view in 1946.

PABLO PICASSO

The Gobbler of Sea Urchins

October 22, 1946
Oil on canvas
130 x 81 cm. (51⅜ x 31⅞ in.)

Picasso's depiction of a fisherman gobbling sea urchins captures the immediacy of the moment. The man bends his head down to meet the spiny shellfish in his right hand, his rubbery limbs marked by an abnormal flexibility. The fisherman, identified by his blue-striped shirt, is an anonymous figure, interesting to Picasso because of the daily life he represents and his small but important role in that life. The simple, sensual pleasure the fisherman derives from "gobbling" the sea urchins strikes a common chord with Picasso's own attitude toward life in 1946: to revel in all that is offered.

The painting is different from the other works reproduced here, in style and media. The solid, thick-limbed figure is reminiscent of the heavy, monumental types that dominated Picasso's art from 1920 through 1923. This "Neoclassical" phase was typified by large, figural forms, often of mythological characters. Picasso turned to this same period for thematic material for the large *Antipolis* paintings, seen on previous pages. But the *Gobbler of Sea Urchins* has another ancestor as well, in the sad *Guitarist* of the Blue Period. The same hunched-over, almost inhuman folding and compacting of the body is common to both works.

Picasso, during the period at Antibes, used mostly plywood or fibro-cement for his paintings because canvas was in short supply. But the *Gobbler* is executed on canvas and the material is used to give a textural effect. Paint is applied thinly over the surface, leaving the coarse weave of the printed linen exposed. The dynamic composition, a combination of line and texture, is carefully planned within the quadrant of the canvas ground. The line flows harmoniously, yet with a strength and unique solidity not found in the other paintings from the Antibes period.

61

PABLO PICASSO

Still Life with Watermelon

1946
Oil and ripolin enamel on plywood
93 x 175 cm. (36⅝ x 68⅞ in.)

Still Life with Bottle, Sea Urchins, Fruit Dish, and Three Apples

1946
Oil on plywood
91 x 209 cm. (35¹³⁄₁₆ x 82¼ in.)

Picasso recorded his view of daily life in a series of large-scale still-life paintings executed at Antibes. The paintings combine traditional and abstract depictions to form sober compositions. The palette is generally dark and calm. Picasso's internal peace and benevolent feeling at the end of World War II caused him to turn again to the tradition of still-life representations. The stable values of this tradition were as attractive to his state of mind as the fantasy of the mythological themes: both express his response to the world's return to a certain normality.

Still Life with Watermelon depicts a knife, glass, bottle, and cut melon on a table. Abstraction is evident in the planar arrangement of the glass at the left and the reduced, cylindrical form of the bottle at the right. In contrast, the knife and melon are more traditionally represented, conveying a sense of homeliness and security in their smooth forms. This extremely large and commanding painting offers an orderly composition of well-balanced elements.

Still Life with Bottle, Sea Urchins, Fruit Dish, and Three Apples is a more abstract work, with an emphasis on sharpness and linearity. The tabletop is tilted up in counter-perspective in order to display its objects. A compote dish with three apples, the red sea urchins, and the triangular-shaped bottle are simple, linear depictions drawn on the surface, lacking plasticity and articulation. The lines of the composition are rhythmic and balanced, and contribute to the overall sense of calm in the large monumental planes.

At Antibes, Picasso eliminated the harsh black outlines that had delineated objects in his still-life paintings of 1945 and early 1946, in favor of smooth planar forms. He became concerned with a clearly rational interpretation of images, echoed in the crisp, clean shapes and lines of this work.

PABLO PICASSO

Owl on a Chair with Sea Urchins

November 6, 1946
Oil and ripolin enamel on plywood
80 x 77 cm. (31½ x 30⁵⁄₁₆ in.)

While Picasso was at Antibes, a friend presented him with an owl that he had found wounded in the street. Picasso became fond of the creature, and kept its cage in his studio day and night; it became his companion while he painted. The bird often perched on a branch or the back of a chair, and for this painting, *Owl on a Chair with Sea Urchins*, it served as a model. Curiously, the impression this owl made on the artist's work was long-lasting. Picasso, steeped in mythology, was not unaware of the mysterious associations of "Athena's bird." This creature of the night appears again and again in his paintings after this first depiction; it became a favorite subject from 1947 on. The owl's features became an obsession to Picasso and appear in the volumetric, triangular bodies and glinting round eyes of later drawings of people. Even the *Gobbler of Sea Urchins* (page 61), with his peaked brow and horizontal brow-line, is akin to the owl of Antibes.

Owl on a Chair with Sea Urchins has the quality of a collage in its mixed use of paint on the raw plywood surface. The owl perches on the crossbar of the chair, casting a raking black shadow downward, and a plate of sea urchins rests on the seat. The triangular body of the animal, with its wide, staring eyes and pointed beak, is almost abstract and has a haunting effect. But, like the other paintings of the Antibes period, an underlying feeling of stability is established by the geometric linearity of the composition. Any malevolent spirit is neutralized by the whimsical sea urchins, quaintly rendered in black brushstrokes.

PABLO PICASSO

Woman with Sea Urchins

November 6, 1946
Oil and ripolin enamel on plywood
119 x 83 cm. (46⅞ x 32¹¹⁄₁₆ in.)

The *Woman with Sea Urchins* is another figure from Picasso's daily life at Antibes. Perhaps a figure viewed in the street, she holds a plate of sea urchins. This spiny shellfish was represented repeatedly during Picasso's stay at Antibes. The figure is abstract: a conglomerate of flat surfaces forms the head, and the facial features, while arranged in a pleasing composition, are certainly not naturalistic. An abstract jigsaw pattern of muted colors forms her dress, while blue-stockinged legs shoot out beneath. The sea urchins are sketched in heavy black, much the same as they are represented in the many still lifes and local portraits of 1946. Picasso painted this scene on plywood. The thinly applied paint and porous surface of the wood combine to make each brushstroke visible.

The *Woman with Sea Urchins* was painted on the same day as the *Owl on a Chair with Sea Urchins* (page 65): November 6. Both include sea urchins as a secondary element, perhaps as a reference to the vast ocean spread out below the Grimaldi Palace. In many ways, the "portrait" of the owl is repeated in the portrait of the woman; similarities include the triangular shape of the body, prominent nose, and wide, pin-dotted eyes. However, even though both were executed on the same day, Picasso worked in different artistic styles. The *Woman* looks back to Cubism in the abstract rearrangement of her face and figure, while the *Owl* retains a more traditional and recognizable form. Both compositions have a delight and charm; their fantasy is typical of Picasso's paintings of 1946.

Musée National Fernand Léger, Biot

FERNAND LEGER

b. Argentan, 1881
d. Gif-sur-Yvette, 1955

The Face at the Window

Ca. 1950
Watercolor with pencil on paper
33 x 25 cm. (13 x 9⅞ in.)

In 1939, Fernand Léger immigrated to the United States, where he spent the war years, returning to France in 1945. During these years, he taught at Yale University and other colleges. Artistically, an "American phase" as such is not evident in his work and Léger himself continually insisted that his work remained consistent. However, he was not indifferent to the new scene that surrounded him.

Léger related an experience he had in New York: "In 1942, in the streets of New York—on Broadway to be exact—I was struck by the colored lights that the advertisements flash on the street. I was talking with someone. His face was blue; twenty seconds later it turned yellow. That color went, another came, and it turned red, then green. I raised my eyes and looked at the buildings. They were sawed in colored strips. I was greatly impressed. That color, the color of the flashing lights, was free—free in space. I tried to do the same thing in my pictures."

The Face at the Window is one of many works inspired by this experience on Broadway. Against the linear contours of a woman's face, broad bands of color, blue, red, and yellow, sweep across the page. As Léger himself stated, the color is separated completely from the design, giving the drawing a "quite different movement, an intense dynamism." The separation of color and the value of color as an independent element is an integral aspect of Léger's work. The strips of pigment cut across the black lines of the figure to create powerful contrast in the composition.

The relationship of color to line as seen in *The Face at the Window* was used only sporadically in Léger's art during the last twenty years of his life. Major late works such as *The Great Parade* of 1954 and *The Country Outing* of 1954 (page 95) distinctively use this concept of color independent of line.

FERNAND LEGER

Study for "The Woman in Blue"

1912
Oil on canvas
132 x 99 cm. (52 x 39 in.)

Fernand Léger, in the early part of his career, was a member of the Cubist circle in Paris. Cubism, initiated by Picasso, Braque, the poet Guillaume Apollinaire, and others, was in opposition to the Impressionist style. The Cubist style in painting countered the characteristic "light without form" technique of the Impressionists with an insistence on volume, structure, and three-dimensionality. Léger became acquainted with Cubist principles through his friendship with Robert Delaunay, through the work of Picasso and Braque, and, after the 1910 Salon d'Automne, through other artists as well.

In the spring of 1911, Léger exhibited a large canvas, *Nudes in a Forest*; its cylindrical, powerful forms are typical of early, geometric Cubism. Between 1911 and 1913, Léger's application of Cubist structure shifted from the simple massive shapes represented in *Nudes* to a more coloristic, nondescriptive mode. In 1911, he painted *The Marriage*, which introduced a number of innovations into his work: more abstract, purely pictorial elements and an independence from the direct observation of a specific subject. In February 1912, the Futurists held their first exhibition in Paris in which they virtually attacked the Cubists for the traditional quality of their subject matter. In reaction to this challenge, Léger painted the *Woman in Blue*.

Study for "The Woman in Blue," executed in 1912, reflects the same basic concerns found in *The Marriage*, a painting of 1911—concerns which he later refined in the final canvas. The work depicts a woman dressed in blue, seated at a table; a cup rests on the table. This is an extremely traditional subject, one which has a long history in French painting. More immediately, it refers to a favorite subject of Cézanne: *Woman with a Coffee Pot*. Cézanne had had a decisive influence on Léger's early works. However, with *Woman in Blue*, Léger broke from the example of the Post-Impressionist master by further developing the innovations he had introduced in *Marriage*—emphasizing a greater degree of abstraction that ultimately led to the total submergence of the subject. In *Woman in Blue*, pure color elements are intensified and the flat blue areas of the model's dress lose their descriptive function, becoming abstract in their flatness. The light, prismatic colors range from grey-white to deep blue with heavy black outlines defining the forms. This small study differs somewhat from the final picture; here the planes are more fragmented and contrasts are more hard-edged. In the final version, the pictorial contrasts are heightened and the image of the woman is further clarified—a tendency toward description which dominates Léger's subsequent paintings. *Woman in Blue*, in both its preparatory and final versions, presents in painted form Guillaume Apollinaire's statement: "The subject no longer counts and if it does, it is against the will of the painter."

In 1954 Léger, looking back on his 1912–13 activity, recalled it as a "battle of liberation from Cézanne. [His] grip was so strong that to get free of it, I had to go as far as abstraction. Ultimately, in the *Woman in Blue* . . . I felt that I had freed myself from Cézanne."

70

71

FERNAND LEGER

Women with Flowers

1921
Oil on canvas
73 x 92 cm. (28³/₄ x 36³/₁₆ in.)

The Big Barge

1923
Oil on canvas
125 x 190 cm. (49¹/₄ x 74³/₄ in.)

In the early 1920s Léger practiced two major styles: a mechanical style that was infused with the spirit of machines and industry, and a classical, monumental figure style. Both are characterized by a streamlined compositional clarity, although the emphasis remains on purely pictorial effect. As he stated in a March 1922 letter to Léonce Rosenberg, Léger sought to achieve "maximum pictorial realization by means of plastic contrasts." And indeed, figures and landscapes are defined solely by modelling, rounded contours, and unexpectedly flat areas of pure color.

In this Léger reflected the rising trends in Parisian modernism, particularly the ideas of the Purist movement started in 1918 by Le Corbusier and Amédée Ozenfant with their publication *Après le Cubisme*. The ideas of this publication were revived in 1920 in the influential journal, *L'Esprit Nouveau*, which advocated an architectonic simplicity in all the arts, heralding the machine aesthetic as the way to the future. Léger met Corbusier in 1920 and was immediately attracted to his theories. Following Corbusier's example, Léger concluded that color had "architectural value, social function, and psychological influence." This emphasis on color is revealed in the flat, unmodelled planes of the two paintings reproduced here.

Women with Flowers is one of several paintings executed in the "classical" style of 1921–24, a style most successfully employed in *The Luncheon* of 1923. It is usually considered a study for that monumental composition. As with *Woman in Blue* of 1912, Léger relied on traditional subject matter, here depicting three women in an interior. Two are clothed in brilliant primary reds and blues, while the third reclines nude on a couch. The composition can be linked to the classical figures of Picasso's paintings after 1919. Another notable influence is that of northern "primitive" painters of the fifteenth century, whose disparate perspective devices were used to advantage by Léger and the Purists. The blank, standardized expressions of the women convey an anonymous, mechanized quality. The overall effect is one of "products on a conveyor belt," and is not far removed from the industrialized landscapes that Léger was also painting at this time.

In *The Big Barge*, Léger has focused on the object and has painted it with directness and simplicity. He has depicted the reality of modern life on the Seine just outside of Paris. This scene is far removed from the peaceful Normandy countryside that characterized his earlier landscapes, including the first version of this work, *The Barge* of 1920. The movement of the barge is indicated by the sharp, angled planes, yet this movement is carefully controlled. Control is a key to this composition that so utterly lacks spontaneity and freedom; the abundant number of preliminary studies to this final canvas testify to its calculation and measure. *The Big Barge*, in its reflection of Purist thought, is a view of life in the machine age, expressing the "beauty" of industry and progress in its factory-dotted landscape. Similarly, *Women with Flowers* must be seen as a reflection of the *esprit nouveau* view of modern life, its monumental women giving a classical, timeless quality to the modernity of mechanization.

73

FERNAND LEGER

Mona Lisa with Keys

1930
Oil on canvas
73 x 92 cm. (28³/₄ x 36³/₁₆ in.)

In 1927, Fernand Léger began a series of compositions which he called "*objets dans l'espace.*" These paintings concentrated on the juxtaposition of unrelated objects in space. The *Mona Lisa with Keys* of 1930 is representative of this new style, truly placing objects in the air. Represented in the relatively small picture are a bunch of keys surrounded by a hazy reproduction of the *Mona Lisa*, a tin of sardines, and a circular form. All are underscored by a semicircle of black ribbon that ties the free-floating forms together.

Léger described how he came to paint the canvas: "In 1928 or 1930, I found a drawing, an exact copy, of a bunch of keys. I was very interested at this point in contrasting objects in space. I asked myself the question: what object is most opposed to a bunch of keys? I thought: the face of a woman, the body of a woman. I went out and, in a window, saw a postcard of the *Mona Lisa*. I said to myself: this is it. But is it possible? In opposing a bunch of keys and, at the top of the canvas, a can of sardines. I composed the final painting from the point of view of juxtaposing objects. For me, the *Mona Lisa* is merely an object like any other."

In the 1920s, Léger abandoned the abstract Cubism for such works as *Woman in Blue* (page 71) to focus on these images of isolated objects. Flat architectural planes and pure color tones prevailed over the earlier volumetric shapes. Between 1925 and 1926, this new technique resulted in still lifes of pipes, roses, bottles, cords, and playing card figures. These same forms were picked up a year later in the "objects in space" series. Certain shapes can also be traced to earlier works: for example, the circular form in the *Mona Lisa with Keys* repeats the contours depicted in *The Disks* of 1918.

The connection between the "objects in space" series and the Surrealist movement cannot be ignored. The floating, ethereal quality of the face of the Mona Lisa has caused some critics to cite Surrealist influences in Léger's art. In 1924, André Breton had published his *Surrealist Manifesto*, discussing, among other ideas, the collection of images brought together in an irrational manner. Certain features of the *Mona Lisa with Keys*, such as the smoky yellow cloud pillowing the composition and the lazy interplay of forms, lend a dreamlike aspect to the painting. In another work of this series, *Umbrella with Keys* (1932), the eccentric writer Lautréamont's scene of a chance meeting between an umbrella and a sewing machine is evoked. However, though Léger may have borrowed elements from the Surrealists, his ideology is purely his own, more concerned with the equality of objects than with potential irrationality. In comparison to Marcel Duchamp's iconoclastic use of the *Mona Lisa* in 1919, in which he drew a mustache on a reproduction of the venerated painting, Léger merely presents the famous image as an object, like any other object, with no more value than the keys, can of sardines, or ribbon.

75

FERNAND LEGER

Study for "The Three Musicians"

1930
Oil on canvas
73 x 92 cm. (28³⁄₄ x 36³⁄₁₆ in.)

The Three Musicians was the subject of a group of drawings, studies, and paintings by Léger. The first drawing was executed in 1925, inspired by a street band on the rue de Lappe in Paris. The final painting, done in America in 1944, was imbued with a vibrancy which Léger declared would have been "less intense and colder if it had been painted in France." The *Three Musicians* theme survived the final painting to appear as a minor motif in later works, for example, in *The Great Parade* of 1954.

Léger was probably familiar with Picasso's two renditions of the subject, done in 1921, both large compositions executed in the abstract, fragmented manner of Synthetic Cubism. Léger instead uses a straight-forward manner to depict an identifiable group of three figures holding an accordion, trombone, and bass, knit together in a tight square. The faces of the men are expressionless, stamped from a common mold, and though each one is distinguished by individualizing characteristics, all three remain without personalities.

Léger was interested in the anonymous worker (or even musician) and here represents him with humor and simplicity. The "Sunday best" clothes of the three performers are drawn sparingly in black line with a hint of color and shade. The stereotypical, popular view is emphasized by the paper cutout effect of the group against the blank ground. Perspective in the painting is undermined by the two-dimensionality of the musicians' chairs, much the same way that the figures of Léger's "classical" paintings defied spatial continuity through the contrast of flat planes.

The *Three Musicians* series explored the theme of a group of men at work, performing their mundane task with neither enthusiasm nor dislike. An effect of naivete is conveyed by their blank acceptance of their task, an acceptance common to most workers, and an attitude continually fascinating to Fernand Léger.

FERNAND LEGER

The Four Cyclists

1943–48
Oil on canvas
130 x 162 cm. (51$^3/_{16}$ x 63$^3/_4$ in.)

The bicycle is a favorite object in the paintings of Fernand Léger in the 1940s, as was a bunch of keys in the 1930s. *The Four Cyclists* is one of several paintings which represent this theme. The mundane, somewhat hackneyed subject is four women on a bicycle outing. The robust, standardized figures are given no more attention than their bicycles; instead, Léger stresses the relationship of man to machine. The composition is a mass of interlaced bodies and bicycles, yet the underlying force of the women is conveyed in their hefty limbs and blank, inscrutable faces. Léger remarked: "There they are, my 'Beautiful Cyclists,' with Big Julie in the middle. Health, life, forms, colors. They spew out the dust of the office or factory and drink in the air of the open country. One can build something with forces like those."

The composition is a confrontation between the two-dimensional and the three-dimensional. The linear forms of the four figures are rounded with contoured shading but, against the flat planes of the background, they lack corporeality. The entire painting is essentially a network of contrasts, with bands of color weaving in and out of the anchoring lines. They pass in waves over the face, arms, and bodies, leaving them unchanged, and their independence only serves to emphasize the heavy linear contours.

The bicycle theme is repeated in several of Léger's paintings, including *Big Julie*, *Two Cyclists*, and *Homage to Louis David*. The family-portrait effect of this last painting is derived from the hefty figures of *The Four Cyclists*, who, with their simple method of transportation, present a working-class social image.

FERNAND LEGER

The Builders

1950
Oil on canvas
300 x 228 cm. (118$\frac{1}{8}$ x 89$\frac{3}{4}$ in.)

The theme of construction workers dominated Léger's art between 1950 and 1951. Numerous drawings and preliminary studies, including details of figures, machines, and even hands, trace the development of the composition from as early as 1940. The final state of the theme, executed in 1950 and reproduced here, depicts an interplay of steel girders and active figures in a large composition. The focus on industrialization is reminiscent of Léger's earlier paintings, yet he also draws on his conception of the human figure as an object. Here, the figure has evolved to take on personal, distinctive characteristics, shedding the automated image of the monumental style of the 1920s. The relative individuality of the men can be detected in the group at the left corner: their horizontal arrangement parallels the steel girder they hold, yet their distinctive features offer the sharp contrast Léger loved. Léger described how he came to paint this work:

> When I executed *The Builders*, I did not make a single plastic concession. I got the idea travelling to Chevreuse by road every evening. A factory was under construction in the fields there. I saw the men swaying high up on the steel girders! I saw man like a flea; he seemed lost in his inventions with the sky above him. I wanted to render that: the contrast between man and his inventions, between the worker and all that metal architecture, that hardness, that ironwork, those bolts and rivets. The clouds, too, I arranged technically, but they form a contrast with the girders. No concession to sentimentality, even if my figures are more varied and individual. I try to do something new without leaving aside the problem. In my work, humanity has evolved like the sky. I set more store on the existence of the people but at the same time I control their actions and their passions. I think that in this way truth is expressed better, more directly, more durably. The anecdote ages quickly."

After its completion, Léger hung *The Builders* in the lunchroom of the Renault automobile factory. To his surprise and disappointment, the workers were indifferent to the painting. However, when one man remarked to the artist that the workers would realize, once the picture was removed, what was in his colors, Léger was gratified. He was deeply concerned with the social value of art and created his paintings for all mankind. The impact of this particular painting extended into other arts: Paul Eluard dedicated his poem *Les Constructeurs* to Léger, and in 1956 Georges Bauquer translated Léger's image into film with *Les Constructeurs*.

The painting is rendered in brilliant yet extremely harsh colors: electric blue, orange-red, tawny yellow. These are the same primary colors found consistently in Léger's work, yet here they are no longer "pure." The violence of the colors and the composition's slashing verticals and horizontals and ramming diagonals serve to evoke the reality of the industrialized twentieth century.

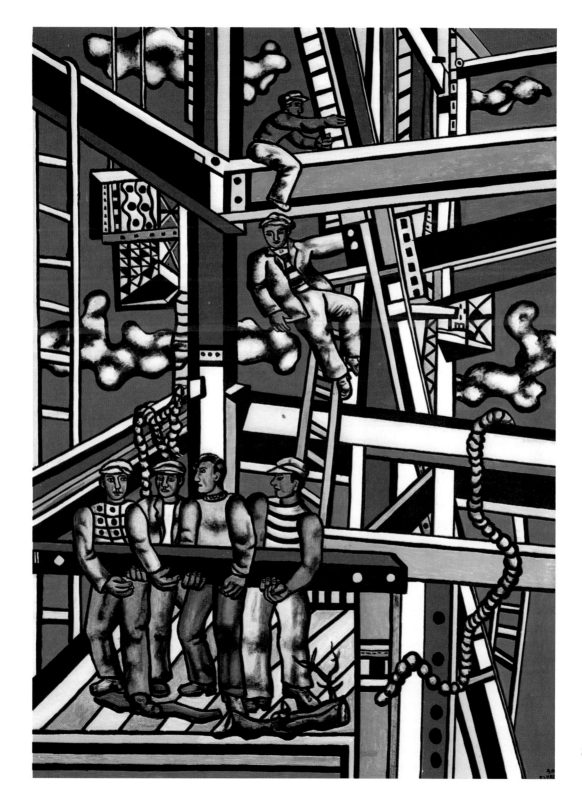

81

FERNAND LEGER

Two Mosaics:
   Woman with a Bird
   Two Nudes (Mother and
      Child)

1950
Ceramic polychromed mosaic
230 x 140 cm. (90⁹/₁₆ x 55¹/₈ in.)
   220 x 130 cm. (86⅝ x 51³/₁₆ in.)

In 1924, Léger, with his friend Léonce Rosenberg, visited the ancient Byzantine city of Ravenna in Italy. There they saw the famous mosaics which date to the time of Justinian (sixth century AD). Léger's interest in mosaics was a long-lasting one and is reflected in his work, from the flat, architectural still lifes of the 1920s to the ceramic mosaics of the 1950s. A parallel to mosaics can be seen in Léger's so-called "Surrealist" works of the 1930s, such as the *Mona Lisa with Keys* (page 75): the ethereal, floating composition of objects is reminiscent of the weightless, otherworldly quality of the Ravenna mosaics. Mosaic technique was brought to Parisian attention by the Purists, who in 1920 reproduced mosaics from the Roman Baths of Caracalla in their journal, *L'Esprit Nouveau.*

In 1949, Léger began to produce ceramics at Biot, a village in southern France, where one of his former pupils, Roland Brice, allowed him the use of his kilns. Picasso had begun working with ceramics that same year at Vallauris, and Chagall, in Vence, was also working in the medium. The Côte d'Azur was once again becoming the artistic center it had been for the Fauves. At this time, Léger was fascinated with constructed form and experimented with ceramic mosaic, bas-reliefs, and three-dimensional sculpture.

The two mosaics at Biot were most likely produced in the 1950s and are based on earlier compositions. *Woman with a Bird* is seen in a 1952 gouache. The monumental female figure is heavily outlined in black with shades of grey, suggesting a certain roundness and plasticity. Yet the flat, brilliant red ground (akin to the gold grounds at Ravenna) negates any effect of three-dimensionality that the contours may suggest. The figure therefore appears to hang in the air against an indeterminate ground.

Two Nudes (Mother and Child) is after a 1923 painting of the same title, one in Léger's series of "classical" paintings of the early 1920s. That work was in turn preceded by an oil study and a drawing, demonstrating Léger's frequent reuse of figures and motifs throughout his career. Again the subject is traditional. In comparison to compositions rendered in the early 1920s, the painted version of *Two Nudes* adopted a simpler spatial solution, which made it ideally suited for the bold simplicity of mosaics. The curvilinear forms of the mosaic are placed in direct contrast to the anonymity of the grey background. The influence of Roman mosaics that marked the artist's earlier compositions is fully realized in *Woman with a Bird* and *Two Nudes.* Here, he employs not only the pictorial effect of mosaics, but the actual medium as well. Léger executed monumental mosaics in the 1950s for the Chapelle d'Assy in Haute Savoie, and for the University of Caracas, and one decorates the facade of the Léger Museum at Biot.

 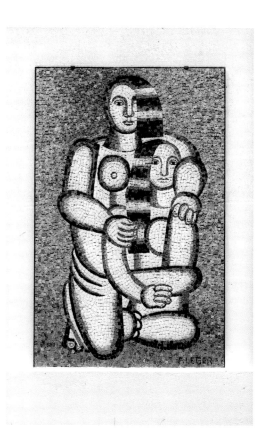

83

FERNAND LEGER

The Children's Garden

1950s
Polychromed ceramic
800 cm. high (314½ in.)

In the 1950s, Léger devoted much time to his ceramic studio at Biot in southern France, and produced some notable three-dimensional sculpture during this period. In these extremely plastic works, Léger's aim was to associate the technique of the potter with the art of the sculptor, imposing on the terra cotta medium the dynamic line of constructed form. Typical of this phase is the monumental ceramic sculpture, *The Children's Garden*, which explores the possibilities of color in space. The large-scale, biomorphic forms are composed in fantastic, undulating shapes and bright, primary colors. These forms first appeared in Léger's landscapes of the 1930s, and the same organic trees and plant shapes are found in the *Butterfly and Flower* of 1936. In *Garden*, color again takes a major role in delineating the flat surfaces cleanly and without modelling. The forms are constructed of pieced-together blocks that reflect Léger's continuing interest in the art of mosaic, and in creating line with chunks of material. One could almost call this sculpture, with its giant, uneven "tesserae," a mosaic construction.

The immense size of the bulbous forms suggests magnification. Léger is considered one of the few modern artists (along with Paul Klee and Franz Marc) to realize the value of the microscope and the dependence of the twentieth-century artistic view on magnification. The sculpture is polychromed in bold reds, blues, and yellows, reflecting in its simplicity the title, *The Children's Garden*.

In an introduction to an exhibition catalogue of his polychromed sculptures, Léger wrote in 1953 that his sculpture marked an evolution of his art toward a final cooperation with architecture. "The last stage is in progress. . . . We have had many technical difficulties yet they have been resolved always keeping to the principles of contrasts. Because the reason for all my work has been to contrast."

FERNAND LEGER

Women with a Parrot

Ca. 1940
Stained glass
200 x 300 cm. (78³/₄ x 118¹/₈ in.)

In the medium of stained glass, Fernand Léger found a suitable material for his "decorative" compositions—one dependent on two basic elements, line and color. Léger set distinctions between decorative art, mural art, and easel painting: the decorative always changes according to taste; it is not necessarily figurative; and it can only exist in the free play of colors. Frescoes, mosaics, and stained glass are not part of the wall, but merely decorate it.

In his late years, Léger received numerous commissions for large-scale murals, mosaics, sculpture, and stained glass. He designed windows for the church of Audincourt in 1951 and in 1954, windows for the church of Courfaivre in Switzerland, and for the University of Caracas in Venezuela. Léger found designing stained glass sympathetic to his aesthetic interests. The heavy, black lines characteristic of his paintings take on a functional aspect in stained glass, since they hold the glass in place. Color, the other major element in Léger's art, becomes raidant and evocative when aided by light, as in the windows of Chartres Cathedral. In Léger's windows color reserves its right as an independent element sweeping across the linear scheme.

Women with a Parrot was also produced as a ceramic sculpture in 1952 under the guidance of Roland Brice. The actual window was made by Aubert and Pitteloup, master glassmakers of Lausanne. The scene depicts three women in a country landscape. Trees burst forth with branches, and leaves are scattered randomly. A large parrot hovers near the center. One figure is seated on a fence at the right while the other two are half hidden in the riotous play of lines. The overall effect is one of gaiety. The areas of color are isolated, flowing independently, yet the harmony of this flow serves to balance the composition.

In his late works, Léger was still concerned with creating a collective view of modern life. The pleasant ambience of such paintings as *The Country Outing* (page 95) and *Women with a Parrot* is merely one aspect of Léger's view of modern life: "An epoch of contrasts, a life of fragments. Our countrysides which were once melodious are bursting with metallic geometry which rises everywhere to hold the clouds. The multicolored billboard of the grey village, the tiny travellers lost in the maze of iron architecture. Our paintings are real if they represent this visual evolution."

In his art, Léger attempted to depict the contrasts and fragments of life. They are perhaps fully realized in the stained-glass window, *Women with a Parrot*.

The Fondation Maeght, St.-Paul de Vence

POL BURY

b. Haine-St.-Pierre, Belgium, 1922

Fountain

1978
Stainless steel
230 x 410 x 270 cm. (90½ x
106¼ in.)

No photograph of Pol Bury's *Fountain* can convey the impact and drama of this work, for almost half of the fountain is in constant motion. Nodding, dipping, rising, bobbing, the metal branches that serve as spigots move with a fluidity that is a perfect complement to the flowing action of the water. This movement appears both random and magical, as there is no visible machinery controlling the orbit of the branches. Only close examination reveals Bury's method: each branch is a carefully balanced cylinder; as it fills with water from below, it tips forward until its contents spill out in a smooth stream; once empty it returns to its original position.

Motion has been a constant factor in Bury's mature works. In 1952 he visited an exhibition of Calder's mobiles and recalled the event as "a great door opening for me." Within a year he began to produce sculptures which could be set in motion by hand, later developing more sophisticated mechanized pieces. By the mid-1950s, Bury was recognized as one of the leading exponents of Kinetic art, that is, art which is dependent on movement, actual or optical.

A recent development in his Kinetic sculptures is his exploration of water in motion. This *Fountain*, installed by Bury, is one of the largest of the series in which water is used as a dynamic element. The shining, reflective, opaque surface of the cylinders serves as a perfect foil for the shining, transparent water: these elements coalesce to form a fluid, mercurial image. This representation of constant flux can be seen as referring to the cycles of nature, but Bury himself is reluctant to stress such analogies. Instead, he emphasizes that movement itself is central to his works: " When they are not moving, they are incomplete. They may be nice shapes, but for me they are not finished sculptures." In *Fountain*, aided by sophisticated construction and the natural forces of gravity and water, Bury has transformed and completed his sculpture through motion. It is this added aspect of Bury's art that is most beguiling to the viewer. In constant activity, *Fountain* carries on its performance in the gardens of the Fondation Maeght, where it continues to conquer immobility.

MARC CHAGALL

b. Vitebsk, Russia, 1889

Life

1964
Oil on canvas
296 x 408 cm. (116½ x 160⅝ in.)

The year that this painting was made, Chagall also received a commission to create a new ceiling for the Opera House in Paris. The vastness of that project finds its painterly equivalent in the Fondation Maeght canvas seen here. Indeed, Chagall spent much of his time on large-scale projects; early in his career he worked with the set designer Léon Bakst; later he designed a curtain and costumes for the *Firebird* ballet in New York, as well as a series of stained-glass windows, and several mosaic walls. Despite their monumental size, these public works never lose their intimate and highly personal character. Chagall is famous for the appealing nature of his art: circus imagery, effervescent colors, romantic lovers, folklore, and easily recognized symbolism fill his scenes. However, these motifs mask the radical compositional technique and the truly individual style that Chagall has developed.

Marc Chagall was born in a small Hasidic community in Russia, and the Jewish rites and ceremonies of his childhood are a constant theme throughout his oeuvre. As a young man, he travelled to St. Petersburg to study art, and from there went to Paris. Chagall recalls his first impressions of that city: "At that time the sun of art shone in Paris alone, and even today it seems to me that there is no greater revolution of the eye than that I came across on arriving in Paris in 1910." Chagall rapidly assimilated the tenets of modernism, studying the Impressionists, the Post-Impressionists, the Symbolists, and his contemporaries in the avant garde. Out of these influences he evolved a personal style, combining folklore and fantastic imagery with the structure of Cubism. His colors and imagery are derived from that branch of Symbolism represented by Van Gogh and Gauguin; the flattened space and abrupt juxtaposition and distortion of images are due to the example set by the Cubists—Robert Delaunay in particular.

Life is a review of Chagall's own life and beliefs. A large cosmic wheel dominates the composition, emblematic of the passage of time. Instead of the usual figures of the zodiac, this wheel has a fish, a horse, a violinist, and a nude. Equally unexpected is the figure on the ladder, whose head is replaced by a chicken. On the left are scenes from Chagall's childhood, in the center a view of Paris. Lovers float toward a family; acrobats tumble; musicians play; nymphs and satyrs frolic. And on the far right stands the artist, protected by his winged muse. It is not possible to decipher all this imagery, nor is it necessary. The painting presents the viewer with a vast panorama of life seen through the eyes of an artist. The figures are thrown out of their natural context, overlapping and responding to each other at the whim of their creator. *Life* represents the subjective view of memory. Chagall draws together all these elements from his past, arranging them, despite contradiction and repetition, into a great, celebratory pageant. As he has said: "There is no such thing as progress, there is nothing to regret. There is only your life, which you put into your work."

91

WASSILY KANDINSKY

b. Moscow, 1866
d. Neuilly-sur-Seine, 1944

The Red Knot

1936
Oil on canvas
89 x 116 cm. (35 x 45⅝ in.)

This painting, made late in the artist's career, exemplifies Kandinsky's concern with harmonic composition. The red knot of the title makes a graceful arabesque across the center of the canvas, linking the more emphatic images on either side. While none of the colors in this painting are brilliant in themselves, Kandinsky juxtaposes them carefully, to heighten their effect through calculated contrasts. The same can be said for the many patterns that animate the composition: through contrast they generate energy. With works such as this, Kandinsky puts into practice the compositional theories that he evolved at various stages of his development.

Kandinsky, more than any other artist of his generation, was concerned with developing a nonobjective art; that is, an art that is not merely abstract, but devoid of all reference to objects or concrete images. Instead, Kandinsky believed that it was possible to organize his compositions in purely formal terms without losing any of the qualities that are the basis of art. Indeed, Kandinsky believed that in nonobjective art the principles of color relationships, structure, line, and spiritual content would be more clearly perceived. He frequently cited music as an example for painting to follow, adapting the principles of musical composition to his own work.

He was born in Moscow, and the traditions of Eastern Orthodoxy and mysticism had a deep influence on his painting. His childhood in Odessa provided him with a rich knowledge of Russian culture, and his travels to northeastern Russia in 1889 introduced him to Russian folk art and woodcuts. Kandinsky decided to pursue an artistic career in 1896 and moved to Munich. His first mature paintings, of about 1900, through those of 1910 were primarily landscapes, but as his work developed he allowed his freely rendered compositions and expressive colors a more independent role, liberating them from their descriptive function. He returned to Moscow during the First World War, and after the Russian Revolution became involved in several public art programs. At that time, he came under the influence of the Russian Constructivist movement, which shared many of his views concerning nonobjective art.

Kandinsky returned to Germany in 1922 to work at the Bauhaus, and in 1933 he moved to Paris. *The Red Knot* belongs to this last period spent in France. The variety of colors and patterns recalls his early Expressionist works, while the hard edges of his forms demonstrate his continued interest in Constructivism. The painting can be seen as divided into major and minor themes: greater degrees of color are played against lesser ones; larger forms are elaborated by more delicate patterns and decorations. The composition is harmonic, given dynamism through the interaction of these themes. Through counterpoint, contrast, and balance, Kandinsky orchestrates the disparate parts into a symphonic whole.

FERNAND LEGER

b. Argentan, 1881
d. Gif-sur-Yvette, 1955

The Country Outing

1954
Oil on canvas
240 x 300 cm. (94½ x 118 in.)

Fernand Léger, along with Picasso and Braque, has always been recognized as one of the leaders of the Cubist movement. He was initially trained in architecture, and when he first arrived in Paris in 1900 he earned his living as a drafting assistant in an architectural firm. Léger began to study art in Paris in late 1903. His architectural training informed his art from the first; a concern for space, volume, and clean delineation has consistently dominated his work. He began to receive public notice when he exhibited his *Nudes in the Forest* of 1910 in the Salon des Indépendants of the following year. Like Picasso and Braque, Léger was interested in the fragmentation of form, but his emphasis on the weight and volume of his forms distinguished him from his colleagues. His work grew rapidly more abstract and sophisticated up to the advent of World War I, when he enlisted in the Engineers. He later recalled, in 1949, how his experiences in the trenches transformed his approach to art:

> I left Paris in a period of abstraction, of pictorial liberation. Without any transition I found myself shoulder to shoulder with the entire French nation. . . . That is just what it took to make me forget the abstract art of 1912–13 . . . . Since I got my teeth into that reality the object has never left me.

The war thus acted as a caesura in Léger's development; after it he became increasingly interested in "real" subject matter, immediately accessible to both the scholar and the laborer, and never returned to the formalism of his first mature works. *The Country Outing* fulfills Léger's need to represent the real, at the same time presenting the viewer with an idyllic image of leisure. It is a scene easily understood— a family dressed in their Sunday best indulges in that favorite urban pastime, a drive to the country. Their car can be seen in the background, and, as is inevitable on summer weekends, it seems to have broken down.

The theme of a country outing has a venerable history in art going back to Giorgione's *Pastoral Symphony*. A more recent example of the genre is Manet's famous *Luncheon on the Grass* of 1863. Indeed, Léger was well aware of the fact that he was working in the tradition of the Old Masters. He first sketched this scene in 1943, and over the next eleven years executed at least seventeen studies of it before venturing to do the final work. One sees, reviewing the studies, that Léger continually pared down his image. Ultimately he liberated the color from the confines of the forms, so that it takes on an independent role, sweeping across the cartoonlike composition. Despite his constant reworking of the theme, this last version of *The Country Outing* is triumphant in its freshness and simplicity.

94

95

JEAN ARP

b. Strasbourg, 1887
d. Basel, 1966

Giant Pip

1937
Bronze
162 x 125 x 77 cm. (63¾ x
   49¼ x 30¼ in.)

In 1944, Arp published a defense of "concrete art," a term he preferred to "abstraction," speaking for his generation of artists: "We don't want to copy nature. We don't want to reproduce, we want to produce like a plant that produces a fruit. . . . We want to produce directly and not by way of any intermediary." He went on to explain: "Concrete art wants to transform the world. . . . Concrete art is a basic art that grows the stars of peace, love, and poetry in the head and the heart. Wherever concrete art appears, melancholy leaves, dragging along its grey suitcase of black sighs."

This emphasis on the organic and affirmative in art has characterized Arp's oeuvre throughout his career. He was born in Strasbourg, a city in Alsace that has been alternately French and German, depending on the outcome of various wars through the centuries. Arp studied at the Academy there but soon found its rigid approach to art too confining. He left to live in Switzerland, where he concentrated on writing poetry. Gradually, as he later recalled, he began to draw again. "I tried to be 'natural,' in other words, the exact opposite of what the drawing teachers call 'faithful to nature.'" A visit to Paris in 1914 confirmed his desire to draw and sculpt; while there, he met the leaders of the modernist movement: Picasso, Delaunay, Modigliani, and the poet Apollinaire. However, the greatest influence on his developing style was the work of Sophie Taeuber. They met in 1915 in Zurich, where Arp had taken refuge from the chaos and destruction of the First World War. Taeuber's collages and tapestries set an example of rhythmic, spontaneous composition and color harmony that deeply impressed him. The following year the two of them joined the nascent Dada movement; in 1921 they married. During this period Arp worked chiefly in relief sculpture made up of jigsaw-like pieces of wood.

Arp began working in fully three-dimensional sculpture in 1930; one of his first successful pieces was a statue entitled *Torso*, done in 1931. Five years later he made the monumental *Giant Seed*, an abstract form that suggested the swelling of a fertile kernel. *Giant Pip*, reproduced here, is a combination of these two works. Its general shape recalls that of *Torso*, while the thrust of each member echoes the theme of burgeoning growth of *Giant Seed*. Arp first modelled the sculpture in limestone, and later cast it in bronze. Of the two versions, the bronze is the more successful. Where stone suggests permanence and immutability, the more workable quality of bronze is better adapted to the evocation of organic growth. The highly polished, smooth surface creates an undulating overall flow, heightening the elastic and unified aspect of the piece. In *Giant Pip*, Arp has represented not the appearance of nature but its essence by giving shape to his understanding of its fundamental flow and tension.

96

OSSIP ZADKINE

b. Smolensk, Russia, 1890
d. Neuilly, France, 1967

Statue for a Garden

1958
Bronze
253 x 112 x 57 cm. (99⅝ x
   44¹⁄₁₆ x 22⁷⁄₁₆)

Two dominant forces in Ossip Zadkine's personality find expression in his oeuvre. The first is political, reflected in such works as his famous monuments protesting the horror of the Second World War: *The Prisoner*, 1943, and *The Destroyed City*, 1948–51. The second is poetical; *Statue for a Garden* (reproduced here) and his many studies of Orpheus are representative of this more intimate aspect of Zadkine's art.

Zadkine was born in Russia and it was during his childhood there that he developed his love of nature; his first conscious memories were of walking through forests that he then believed to be inhabited by wild and unruly spirits. Such experiences left a lasting impression and much of his mature work evokes the many metamorphoses of organic growth. In 1905 he went to England and there began to study art. He returned to Smolensk several times, but by 1909 had settled in Paris, where he studied at the Ecole des Beaux-Arts. Within a few years he had joined the Cubist avant garde, and was particularly influenced by the African sculpture so admired by Picasso and Braque. While he later emerged as an independent artist unassociated with any formal school, Zadkine rarely departed from the compositional lessons he had learned from Picasso's example.

Statue for a Garden, executed several decades after his initial contact with Cubism, still shows a marked debt to the tenets of that movement. The figure appears to be half woman, half foliage, with a clearly feminine torso rising out of the stump and limbs of a tree. Working in the Cubist idiom, Zadkine opens up the figure with large gaps and recesses, and emphasizes profiles for dramatic effect. He avoids the traditional rounded volumes of sculpture; instead, *Statue* is made up of a series of complementary concave and convex surfaces. But unlike most Cubist sculptors, Zadkine devotes special attention to the varied textures of the surface, which in this piece range from porous to barklike to smooth.

Despite the high degree of abstraction, both the feminine and the treelike qualities of this work are easily perceived. Read as a figure, the graceful curve of the neck and breasts is unmistakable. Read as a tree, the texture of the bark and the positioning of the branches predominate. It is possible that Zadkine meant this work to suggest the Classical Greek myth of Daphne, a nymph who was transformed into a tree to escape the amorous pursuit of Apollo. This interpretation seems particularly appropriate in view of Zadkine's regular use of Classical mythology for inspiration, and his love of the changing aspect of nature. Furthermore, the metamorphosis of Daphne is a traditionally popular subject for garden sculpture. Thus Zadkine provides a modern equivalent to a venerable genre. The organic form of *Statue for a Garden*, its surface modulated to capture light and shadow, its large scale, and its literary allusions make it ideally suited to its natural setting.

ALEXANDER CALDER

b. Philadelphia, 1898
d. New York, 1976

Humptulips (Totem)

1965
Steel and aluminum
250 cm. high (98$^{7}_{16}$ in.)

Calder closes his autobiography with this postscript: "On February 8, 1966, I had a show of *gouaches* at the Galerie Maeght. To embellish this a bit, I applied the old formula stated by Gigitte Maeght—I scratched my head and came up with some tall black pyramidal shapes with mobile festoons on their heads.... For these I took the name TOTEMS."

Humptulips is the largest of these first *Totems*, and they mark an important new direction in Calder's work. Calder must have recognized this change in direction, since he felt the need to expand his autobiography to include these later sculptures.

Calder was born into a family of sculptors in Pennsylvania; his father and grandfather were responsible for many of the public monuments in that state's capital. His early work is a collection of wire figures, a group of which form his famous *Circus*. He built his first mobiles while living in Paris in the early 1930s. Influenced by the pure, rectilinear compositions of Mondrian, Calder explored the possibilities of designing simple, flat shapes that would interact in space. His mobiles were variously activated by cranks, motors, and, later, wind. The name "mobile" was suggested to Calder by his friend Marcel Duchamp, and Jean Arp baptized Calder's stationary works "stabiles."

To a certain extent the *Totem* sculptures bridge the gap between these two forms. On top of each piece is a light, delicately balanced mobile, while the base is almost a stabile, being much heavier and more substantial than the stands that usually support the mobiles. The name *Totem* is suggestive of sacred, primitive art; since the late 1920s the Surrealists had seized on the imagery of primitive cultures to evoke the basic and primal emotions of the unconscious. While it is unlikely that Calder intended to convey literary and Freudian concerns in his *Totems*, the height and the bold outline of these works are awesome. *Humptulips*, placed at the entry of the Fondation Maeght, has an evocative power that recalls primitive art. The balance between the single black and the many red disks is remarkable; the movement of the mobile forms is slow and natural, caused by wind currents that pass through the courtyard.

These weighty implications are considerably lightened by the title of this piece. At first *Humptulips* appears to be a nonsense word—perhaps descriptive of the shape and brilliant red disks. However, the other pieces of this series are named after cities: *Frisco, Chicago, Pekin*, and, more obscurely, *Foum Tataounie* and *Weekeepeemee*. A glance at the atlas reveals that Humptulips is a town in Washington state. Calder was an inveterate traveller; during much of his life he maintained studios in both France and America. *Humptulips* may be a tribute to a particular place. At the same time the esoteric and ridiculous name reveals Calder's special wit and humor, a sensibility that pervades all his work.

ALBERTO GIACOMETTI

b. Stampa, Switzerland, 1901
d. Chur, Switzerland, 1966

Women of Venice

1956
Bronze
Heights range between 105 cm.
(41¼ in.) and 133.5 cm.
(52½ in.)

In 1922 Alberto Giacometti settled in Paris. After several years of study and independent work, he became allied with André Breton and the Surrealist movement in 1929; this alliance lasted six years. His works of this period have often been classified as "objects" rather than sculptures. These "objects" are curious, almost stagelike constructions made up of assembled elements such as balls, small figures, segments of anatomy, and fantastic forms. In 1935, Giacometti decided to return to a more realist mode, making studies from nature. In a 1947 letter he described how lengthy a process this transition was: "I worked with the model all day from 1935 to 1940."

Giacometti went on to explain that his greatest difficulty in working from the model was that he found himself unable to depict the whole figure, becoming preoccupied with one detail after another. He finally resolved this dilemma by changing his entire approach: instead of direct observation, he relied on his memory. Only through a remembered image was he able to realize the completed figure. These were some of the most difficult years of Giacometti's artistic career. However, this laborious period of working and reworking a single theme resulted in his eloquent and now famous figures of elongated men and women isolated and almost consumed by space.

Women of Venice comprises a group of ten such figures. They were the result of Giacometti's invitation in 1956 to participate in the Venice Biennale, from which they take their title. This series is particularly revealing of Giacometti's method: instead of each figure being created separately, they are all different stages of a single plaster model.

The Giacometti courtyard of the Fondation Maeght offers a rare opportunity to view the work as an ensemble; nine of the ten figures have been brought together here. Most other casts of the sculptures have been split up and scattered to different collections. In the photograph reproduced here, the *Women of Venice* dominate the foreground; later works by the artist appear toward the back. One gets the disquieting sense, walking around these figures, that it is impossible to become truly close to them, however near one may stand. This is partially due to the hermetic stance of the *Women*, each one seemingly drawn into herself, staring straight ahead in the manner of a Cycladic or ancient Egyptian idol. Furthermore, the rough and indistinct modelling of the figures forces the viewer to step back from them in order to see clearly. Only in the overall silhouette is the figure comprehensible; upon close examination the features dissolve. In this fashion Giacometti has achieved something unique in modern sculpture, an existential barrier preventing the viewer from ever breaking the isolation of his figures. The *Women of Venice*, despite the solidity of the bronze of which they are made, remain apparitions, remembered images in a distance that can never be bridged.

103

ALBERTO GIACOMETTI

Monumental Head

1960
Bronze
95 cm. high (37 $\frac{3}{8}$ in.)

Portrait busts are probably the single most frequent theme in Giacometti's oeuvre. His first attempt at sculpture was a bust of his brother Bruno, done when the artist was only thirteen. From that time on, Giacometti experimented with a range of bust types, from barely modelled Cubist and Surrealist heads, to the vividly expressive studies of his brother Diego, to the formal grandeur of *Monumental Head*, reproduced here. In a television interview of 1964 Giacometti stated: "If I ever succeed in realizing a single head, I'll probably give up sculpture. But the funniest thing is, that if I were to do a head as I want to, then probably nobody would be interested in it anymore. . . . What if it were just a banal little head? In fact, since 1935, this is what I've always wanted to do. I've always failed."

While Giacometti may never have attained this ideal, the many busts that he produced during his career attest to his mastery of this genre. Perhaps it is his very need to strive toward an unrealizable goal that makes these works successful, for all his studies of heads are charged with a sense of power and energy which remains intriguingly unresolved.

Unlike many of Giacometti's busts, it is impossible to identify *Monumental Head* with any one sitter. Most of the artist's studies of male heads were modelled after Diego. Other sitters included his wife, Annette, and close friends in the art world. However, *Monumental Head* was intended from its inception to serve a public rather than a private purpose, and this may explain the generalization of its features. In 1958 Giacometti received a commission to execute a series of statues for New York's Chase Manhattan Plaza. Out of this commission evolved three major works: *Monumental Head*, *Standing Woman*, and *Walking Man*.

Giacometti had long been interested in creating a large figure group for public display. In 1932, during his Surrealist period, he produced *Model of a Square*, which is little larger than a chessboard. In this "object" (a term used in preference to "sculpture" to describe Giacometti's Surrealist works) figures are arranged on a white, planar surface, amid totemistic forms. In this fashion Giacometti first explored the possibilities of interrelating figures and space in a unified composition. Later, as he developed his realist figures, he continued to experiment with the theme of figures filling a square, gradually enlarging his work. In late pieces, such as *Monumental Head*, the figure asserts itself over the space. Though little more than twice life size, *Monumental Head* takes on the gargantuan proportions of Roman Imperial statues.

This triumph over space distinguishes *Monumental Head* from much of Giacometti's oeuvre. Unlike *Women of Venice* (page 103), in which the figures appear to be eroding, this bust defiantly dominates its surroundings. It fulfills a public function, and at the same time preserves the personal expression of the artist.

ROBERTO MATTA

b. Santiago, Chile, 1911

Sensible Transparency

1946
Oil on canvas
132 x 92 cm. (52 x 36¼ in.)

In a series of receding planes, Matta draws the viewer into the depths of his painting *Sensible Transparency*. As in much of Matta's work, the evocation and perception of depth is the dominant theme of this canvas. But the visual journey is a frustrated one: the depth suggested by one element is contradicted by another; no single vanishing point unites the composition; the scaffolding that defines the space appears to be on the verge of collapse; and the darkness of the background obscures the focal core of the painting. The structure of the painting is illusory, and has a psychological resonance that is immediately recognizable as a dream reality—a reality that is unstable and violent.

Roberto Matta is one of the most important artists to have joined the Surrealist movement in the late 1930s. Born in Chile, he travelled to Paris in 1933 as an architecture student. There he worked intermittently in the offices of Le Corbusier, but became increasingly interested in painting. In 1937, he met the "Pope" of Surrealism, André Breton, and within a year had begun to produce his first paintings. He was most interested in that aspect of Surrealism which explored the unconscious. However, where the first generation of Surrealists had been concerned with Freudian or poetic images of the unconscious, Matta wished to translate this imagery into the idiom of the new technology of modern machines. His first works, called "psychological morphologies," reflect Matta's concern with charting the unconscious. These are some of his most abstract works; veils of color, applied in a series of washes, dominate them, and strong-hued images emerge through the veils as if they were excavated from the depths of the canvas.

In 1939, he came to the United States and joined the New York circle of European artists in exile, which included Breton, Ernst, Masson, and Marcel Duchamp. Duchamp and Matta became close friends, and the elder artist had a deep influence on Matta's work. Duchamp's famous *Large Glass: The Bride Stripped Bare by her Bachelors, Even* provided twofold inspiration for Matta. The Cubist and Futurist forms, faceted and repeated, of *The Bride* led Matta to emphasize structure in his own paintings, and the transparency of the glass on which the work was painted suggested to Matta a means of opening up this structure by allowing the viewer to look through translucent configurations.

Both these elements are evident in *Sensible Transparency*. Matta often referred to his paintings as "inscapes," that is, landscapes seen by the inner eye. *Transparency* is best understood as such an "inscape," an antirational architecture that reflects a state of mind. Many Surrealists explored this idea of a dream reality; their method was to juxtapose and warp mundane images until they lost their everyday aspect. Matta, in creating his own dream reality in purely formal and abstract terms, gives his "inscapes" a primal universality.

107

WIFREDO LAM

b. Sagua la Grande, Cuba, 1902

The Betrothed of Kiriwina

1949
Oil on canvas
128 x 113.5 cm. (50³/₈ x 44⁵/₈ in.)

Picasso found in primitive art a formal means with which to break from the nineteenth-century traditions of Western painting. Wifredo Lam found in Picasso's art the means to return to the primitive culture of his native Cuba. Where Picasso had discovered something new and different in African masks and totems, Lam saw them as a part of his heritage.

Lam grew up in a small, rural community that was an admixture of various cultures; his ancestry itself is a combination that could only be found on a colonized island. His father was Chinese, his mother of mixed African, Indian, and Spanish origin. Sagua la Grande was a town that maintained traditions of witchcraft, folklore, and voodoo ritual. At the same time, the dictatorial regime of Havana turned to Spain for guidance. The period of Cuban history of Lam's childhood was particularly violent, marked by racism against the Afro-Cuban population.

In 1924, Lam moved to Madrid to study art. A travelling exhibition of Picasso's paintings in 1936 gave him the impetus to turn toward modernism, and after the fall of the Spanish Republic he moved to Paris. There he met Picasso, who was deeply impressed by his work and introduced him to the Paris avant garde. Lam quickly assimilated the tenets of Cubism, adhering to Cubist subject matter as well. André Breton and Surrealism also had a deep influence on his development at this time. It was not until the war forced him to flee France in 1941 in the company of Breton, Ernst, and Matta that he returned to Cuba, and once there he brought his native culture into his art. Recalling that period, Lam said: "I wanted with all my heart to paint the drama of my country, but by thoroughly expressing the Negro spirit, the beauty of the plastic art of the blacks. In this way I could act as a Trojan horse that would spew forth hallucinating figures with the power to surprise, to disturb the dreams of the exploiters."

The Betrothed of Kiriwina realizes Lam's ambition to paint figures with the power to disturb. The figure appears to be part woman, part horned beast, part horse. Her sexuality is emphatic and violent. The rite of marriage has been a frequent theme in Lam's art, but it is seen as almost a brutal sacrifice, rather than as a pacific union. Kiriwina is a town on the small island of Trobriand, off the coast of Papua New Guinea. Lam, with his exploration of primitive cultures, had visited many of the Caribbean islands and studied the rituals of aborigines around the world. New Guinea, with its distance from Western civilization, must have been particularly interesting to him, and in 1928 he had made a study of its native sculpture. However, the artist has appropriated these exotic sources into his own mythic vision. The *Betrothed* depicted here seems waiting to marry some savage god; she herself is inhuman. Lam was able to paint his heritage through the language of Cubism; however, he has given this language a vibrant new vocabulary.

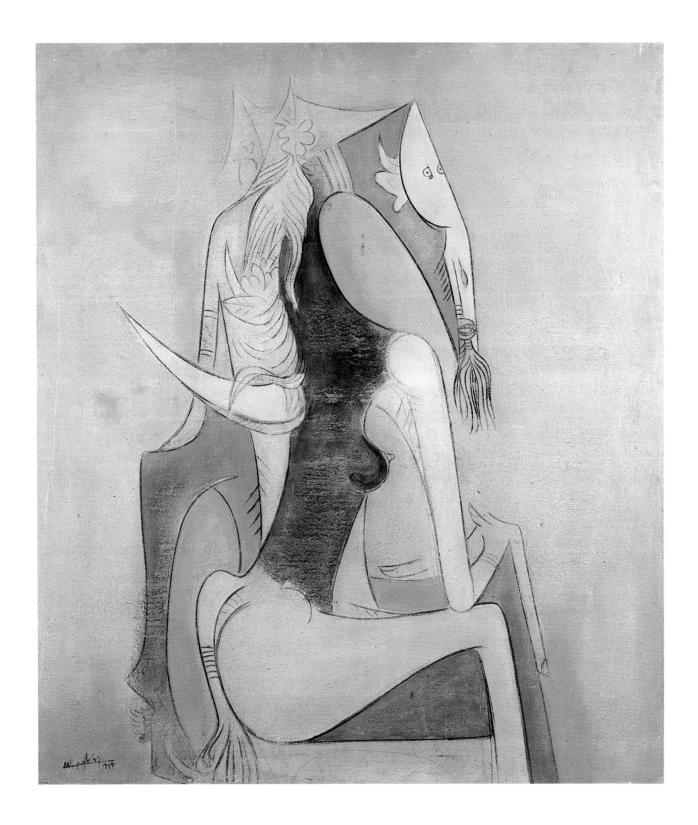

HANS HARTUNG

b. Leipzig, 1904

T 1971 H 13

1971
Acrylic and oil on canvas
154 x 250 cm. (60 $\frac{5}{8}$ x 98 $\frac{7}{16}$ in.)

The desire and search for the absolute is a concern that unifies Hartung's work from his first experimental studies to his most recent canvases. It distinguishes his aims and art from those of his contemporaries, for his work has always fallen outside of the traditonal categories of twentieth-century modernism. In his concern with universal law, Hartung may be linked with the first generation of Northern and Eastern European abstractionists, Kandinsky in particular. In his free, gestural method of painting, he can be allied with the later practitioners of *art informel* in Europe, such as Soulages and Tapiés, and of Abstract Expressionism in the United States, such as Jackson Pollock. However, a close examination of Hartung's career reveals the unique position of this artist.

As a student in Leipzig in 1922, Hartung began a series of watercolors after Van Gogh and Goya, only copying the most general flow of their compositions, omitting all detail. Soon these studies became completely abstract. At the same time, he grew familiar with the work of German Expressionists, admiring their compositions, but finding their imagery excessively literal and distracting. In 1925, he attended a lecture by Wassily Kandinsky and was astonished to discover that there were other artists who were working in a similar nonrepresentational mode. In 1927, he went to Paris and began to assimilate the innovations of Cubism, but by 1935 had purged his work of this highly structural influence and developed a gestural style derived from his first watercolors. After World War II he became a French citizen and moved to the forefront of the Paris avant garde.

Not unlike the American Abstract Expressionists, Hartung views the canvas as a surface to act upon, this action being recorded in paint. It is the gesture that becomes the theme of the painting, rather than any specific image. Hartung stands apart from his American colleagues in that he believes that this gesture should accord with universal laws of order, thus eliminating the sense of improvisation which is central to artists like Pollock. *T 1971 H 13* is an excellent example of Hartung's mature art. (The title is Hartung's private notational system, developed early in his career: T is an abbreviation for *tableau*, 1971 is the year it was painted, and the final number indicates the particular series to which this canvas belongs.) The brilliant primary colors are characteristic of works from this period, as is the black nebula that dominates the center, giving the work an ambiguous sense of space. Despite the freedom of its execution, the composition maintains its balance, as the pull of the bold forms counteract each other. The surface is animated by three types of gesture: the dominant stroke of a wide brush, the crayon-like scribble of nervous lines, and the distant impression left by an airbrush. These gestures merge to form an electric flow; through balance, order is imposed, and Hartung achieves his vision of the unending current of the universe.

110

111

PIERRE SOULAGES

b. Rodez, France, 1919

Painting

1971
Oil on canvas
162 x 130 cm. (63¾ x 51⅛ in.)

Pierre Soulages was forced to start his career as a painter twice. He came to Paris in 1938, but his initial work was soon interrupted by the Second World War. Between 1939 and 1945 he did no painting, but he did come to know and admire the nonrepresentational works of Sonia Delaunay, Wassily Kandinsky, and Piet Mondrian. After the Armistice he moved to the outskirts of Paris and began to paint again. His first abstractions consisted of loose, sweeping lines, but he soon developed his densely structured style, a broad palette knife replacing the brush, a plane of color replacing line.

One of the most cited influences on Soulages's art is the austere Romanesque church of Ste. Foix at Conques, not far from where Soulages was born. Early in his career he displayed an interest in Romanesque architecture, and he has stated that he decided to become a painter during a visit to Ste. Foix. While there is no need to doubt the importance of this influence, it has too often led art critics and historians to identify the strident black lines of his canvases as the massive columns of the church. Actually, the architecture of Ste. Foix had a much more subtle and less literal influence on Soulages, who has always averred that his work is entirely nonrepresentational and has been purged of all naturalistic description. Architecture, instead of providing an image for him to copy, has set an example for Soulages's compositional method. As James Johnson Sweeney noted: "He starts from a single brushstroke, which invites another—this calls up another and another and another until out of their interplay form is born." (*Soulages: Paintings Since 1963*, New York, Knoedler, 1968, p. 8.) The interplay of brushstrokes is densely knit, each part dependent on the whole, much in the same way that a building is dependent on its structure.

This structural approach to nonrepresentational painting distinguishes Soulages from other European abstractionists like Hans Hartung. Hartung's work is also characterized by the painterly gesture (see page 111), but where his gestural strokes seem to float in the infinite space of his canvas, Soulages's are firmly anchored on the surface. Where Hartung experiments with a variety of gestures, colors, and lines, Soulages concentrates on a single, unified image.

The untitled painting reproduced here is an excellent example of Soulages's most recent work. After 1969 he began to open up the structure of his compositions, unifying them by directing his gestural strokes in a harmonious flow, rather than by the strict architectonics of his earlier paintings. The density of the black is alleviated and tempered by the brown stain. The brushstroke is carefully modulated, recalling the subtle sophistication of Oriental calligraphy. Soulages works in only the most painterly method; however, through the austerity of his works he achieves a classicism which allies him with the great traditions of French art.

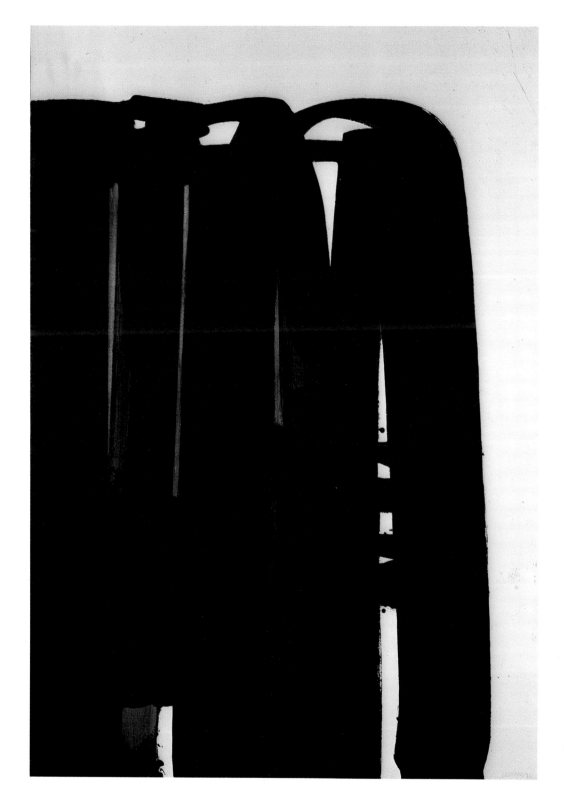

113

PABLO PALAZUELO

b. Madrid, 1918

Omphale II

1962
Oil on canvas
277 x 207 cm. (109 x 81½ in.)

According to a story from Greek mythology, Omphale was a queen of Lydia who figured in the legend of Hercules. After having killed his son, Iphitus, in a blind rage, Hercules was sent to her court for three years of service and penance. Under her influence, he became an effeminate creature, wearing women's clothes and spinning wool among Omphale's maids. Conversely, Omphale took on the hero's lionskin and carried his club. This story of reversed roles finds suitable expression in the abstract painting by Pablo Palazuelo *Omphale II*, second in a series of three works with this title.

As in many of Palazuelo's mature works, the forms in *Omphale II* seem unstable, as if they were about to blend and merge into a new configuration. While *Omphale II* is in no way intended to be read as an illustration of the ancient legend, the overall composition suggests the metamorphosis which is its central theme.

Palazuelo is one of the first Spanish artists of his generation to work in a completely nonrepresentational style. He began painting in 1940, at first following the style of Neo-Cubism, which then dominated European art. Soon thereafter he came under the influence of Kandinsky, Klee, and Mondrian. Indeed, his first nonrepresentational drawings were published in a 1948 *Homage to Paul Klee* produced by the Galeria Palma, in Madrid. Following Klee's example, Palazuelo arrived at his mode of abstraction by studying natural structures: the crystals of a snowflake and monocellular organisms that could only be observed through a microscope. He organized many of his paintings around a central form which seems to radiate energy, pushing the subsidiary shapes beyond the borders of the canvas. By repeating several basic shapes, he gives this movement a sense of rhythm, analogous to that of nature.

However, while Palazuelo may have been inspired by the minutiae of nature, his mature paintings are executed in bold proportions and brilliant color. *Omphale II* is a typical example of his work. In its color, composition, and suggestion of motion and change, *Omphale II* summarizes Palazuelo's aims. In studying nature, Palazuelo has found a fruitful and expressive method of abstraction that is at once powerful and harmonic.

SAM FRANCIS

b. San Mateo, California, 1923

Ariel Coral Free III

1970
Oil on canvas
138 x 183 cm. (54^5/$_{16}$ x 72^1/$_{16}$ in.)

Sam Francis grew up on the West Coast of the United States, in a climate of intense sunlight comparable to that of the South of France. Light fills his canvases, not only in the expanse of white that dominates his works, but in the spectrum of colors he uses as well. Francis once explained that what interested him about light was "not just the play of light, but the substance of which light is made." In accordance with color theory, Francis sees light as made up of the combination of the prismatic colors, and the spectrum as the breakdown of white light into its component parts. While his use of color is intuitive rather than scientific, it results in compositions that seem to radiate white light.

Francis's interest in white light came about during his service in the United States Army Air Corps. In 1941, he suffered a severe spinal injury that forced him to remain on his back for many months. One of the few things that he could focus on was the changing pattern of light on the hospital ceiling. At the same time, he was given a box of watercolors for therapeutic purposes; Francis had never taken a serious interest in art before. By the time he left the hospital, he had decided to become an artist.

His earlier paintings reflect that first experience observing light. They have often been likened to floating clouds or expansive skies. *Ariel Coral Free III*, third in a series, is typical of his more recent work. The colors appear to shift across the canvas; as they blend into each other, the shapes they define become unstable. However, this appearance of instability is counteracted by the brilliance and clarity of the hues. Francis has used pure primary and secondary colors, which remain undiluted in their intensity. At some points the colors bleed into the white; at others, they are hard-edged and clearly delineated. By varying the relationships of the colors, Francis gives *Ariel Coral Free* a sense of motion.

The title of *Ariel Coral Free* is inspired by Shakespeare's *Tempest*, referring to the spirit Ariel's haunting poem:

> Full fathom five thy father lies;
> Of his bones are coral made;
> Those are pearls that were his eyes;
> Nothing of him that doth fade
> But doth suffer a sea change
> Into something rich and strange. (Act I, Scene ii)

Ariel Coral Free is no more an illustration of the play than is Palazuelo's *Omphale* (page 115) of the legend. Rather, Francis is expressing the transience and magic which are the theme of Shakespeare's drama. By exploiting "the substance of which light is made," he has achieved an eloquent clarity and harmony.

117

JOAN MIRÓ

b. Barcelona, 1893

Personage, Bird

1972
Oil and lead on cardboard prepared
  with gouache
105.5 x 75.5 cm. (41½ x 29¾ in.)

Personage, Birds

1976
Ink, oil, and pastel on paper
124 x 81.5 cm. (48¾ x 32$\frac{1}{16}$ in.)

Like his fellow Spaniard Picasso, Joan Miró has been one of the most influential figures in modern art. Drawing on artistic sources from his Catalan background, Miró easily moved into the avant garde when he settled in Paris in 1920. His first works show the influence of Cubist structure and Fauvist color, but he quickly developed an abbreviated, almost symbolic style with paintings like *The Farm*, 1921–22 and *Harlequin's Carnival*, 1924–25. Where many of his contemporaries strove to eliminate narrative from their paintings, Miró developed a unique form of abstraction in which anecdotal elements remained, conveyed by increasingly reduced means. For example, a bird could be represented by an arrowlike line, a face by moustaches.

This form of allusive abstraction made Miró a natural ally of the Surrealists. In 1924, he signed André Breton's first *Surrealist Manifesto*, thus advocating Breton's credo: "Existence is elsewhere." The Surrealists strove to achieve this "elsewhere," a heightened reality, by tapping the subconscious; automatism and free association were employed to release the creative mind from cultural restrictions. Both these methods were ideally suited to Miró's art. In 1925 he painted *The Birth of the World*, which demonstrated a spontaneity of execution unequalled until the advent of Abstract Expressionism. In the early 1930s he experimented with a series of assembled "objects" which brought various articles of daily life into abrupt juxtaposition. While he soon abandoned this form of sculpture, it gave further impetus to his exploration of free association in painting.

A recurrent theme in his oeuvre is the relationship between a figure and birds. The bird can have a variety of meanings within each work, however, it generally refers to a revelatory spirit. The figure usually takes on the role of Everyman, or, as the Surrealists preferred, "*Personnage*."

In the two drawings reproduced here, Miró explores this theme in the vibrant, expressive style of his late works. This style is to a certain extent reminiscent of children's art. The drawing on the left is deceptively casual, with scribbled notations in the margins and apparently indiscriminate layers of color. The personage, either male or female, fills the center, the most distinct feature being a large red eye. To the left of the eye a small triangle represents the bird of the title. The later drawing, on the right, is even more informal; color is spilt on the page quite independently of the drawn figure. The birds are fleetingly described by linear arabesques to the left and bottom of the sheet. Miró maintains order in these drawings through a masterly balance of contrasts. Despite their compositional freedom, the images in these works remain coherent and retain their poetic quality. In both drawings the relationship between personage and bird seems violent and active, instead of passive. Thus Miró treats the bird's revelation of that "elsewhere of existence" (to borrow Breton's phrase) as an exhilarating and perhaps even dangerous experience for the initiate.

JOAN MIRÓ

The Egg

1963
Ceramic
180 cm. high (70$\frac{7}{8}$ in.)

The Mother Goddess

1963
Ceramic
157 cm. high (61$\frac{13}{16}$ in.)

The *Labyrinth* at the Fondation Maeght is one of the most successful examples of artistic collaboration of our century. Joan Miró, the ceramicists Llorens and Joan Artigas, and the architect José Luis Sert worked together to create this intricate sculpture garden. The mythic precedent for this work is Dedalus's maze in Crete, which concealed the legendary Minotaur. The labyrinth at St.-Paul de Vence contains equally strange figures, hybrids that are suggestive of a broad range of poetic imagery.

The association between Sert and Miró originated with the Spanish Pavilion of the 1937 Paris World's Fair. In 1956 Sert designed and built Miró's studio in Palma de Mallorca. Miró's and Llorens Artigas's friendship dates back to their student days in Barcelona, and in 1944 they began to collaborate on a series of ceramic plates. Later, Joan Artigas, Llorens's son, entered this collaboration. In 1962 these four Catalans began to design the *Labyrinth*; their combined efforts resulted in a masterful synthesis of sculpture, architecture, and landscape.

While Miró is primarily known as a painter and graphic artist, he has produced many sculptures. During his association with the Surrealists he made a series of assembled "objects." Following his collaboration with Artigas, Miró became increasingly concerned with plastic and organic pieces, many of which are based on natural forms. On the left of this photograph is Miró's *Egg*. Like many of his works, the genesis of this piece goes back several years. In 1958, he did a series of eggs which range in size from a pebble to fifteen inches. Miró gave this monumental version added significance by inscribing strange ritualistic signs on its surface. The egg is an easily understood image of fertility and birth; the added inscriptions give it the appearance of being a sacred object from a primitive religion. Instead of being just an egg, Miró's sculpture seems to contain the embryo of some great spiritual being. The pool of water that surrounds the piece can be seen two ways: metaphorically, it is the source of all life; visually, it doubles the image through reflection, thus strengthening the allusion to reproduction.

The Mother Goddess, seen on the right, is a much more violent and complex image. Like *The Egg*, it seems to belong to a primitive and ritualistic culture. The title suggests that this is an object to be worshipped. The bloated form suggests fertility, recalling Cycladic votive images, and its sexuality is conveyed by the prominent broad slash down the center and the phallic and breastlike protrusions. Far more mysterious and evocative than *The Egg*, this sculpture is expressive of that part of Surrealist ideology which saw woman as both the great procreator and the castrator of man. The image must have haunted Miró, for he has made many versions of it, large and small, in a variety of media. The juxtaposition of these two sculptures is particularly appropriate. *The Mother Goddess* represents the ineffable and inexplicable aspect of fertility; *The Egg* can be seen as the result.

JOAN MIRÓ

Ceramic

1963
Ceramic
307 x 310 cm. (120⅞ x 122¹⁄₁₆ in.)

The Fork

1963
Steel and bronze
507 cm. high (199¼ in.)

This photograph captures the dramatic interplay between the Fondation Maeght's *Labyrinth* and the surrounding countryside. In the foreground, on the flat terrace, lies Miró's *Ceramic*; in the background, spearing the landscape behind it, stands his *Fork*. Miró's acute visual sensitivity to the site is truly impressive, and to a certain extent he owes this awareness to his first teacher, Francisco Galí, who told his students to go into the mountains around Barcelona "with a crown of eyes around your head."

Ceramic is derived from Miró's mural sculptures. In 1957, following his second period of collaboration with Artigas, the two artists created a vast ceramic mural for the UNESCO building in Paris entitled *Wall of the Moon and Wall of the Sun*. Three years later they undertook a similar project for Harvard University. Both of these murals are made of tiles that were fired by Artigas in his old-fashioned, wood-burning kiln. The brightly colored glazes were also ground by Artigas himself to ensure rich and deep colors not to be found in commercial glass. These traditional methods allowed a certain degree of accident in the firing process, a challenge that stimulated both Miró and Artigas. *Ceramic* is the most abstract of Miró's *Labyrinth* sculptures. It appears to be a segment of a mural, self-contained in its white frame. The brilliant freedom with which the glazes are applied links this piece to the gestural tradition of Abstract Expressionism, and its flat surface allows Miró to introduce his painterly concerns into sculpture. The image is best understood as a kind of abstract sundial. While it does not chart time, the glazed disc captures and refracts the changing light of the Mediterranean sun.

The sharp, profiled form of *The Fork* stands apart from the ceramic works of the *Labyrinth*. The angular simplicity of this piece may be due to the influence of Calder's mobiles (see page 101), and, like Calder's works, the top part pivots according to the direction of the wind. The base is richly textured by rough patches so that the surface seems to be covered with some kind of organic growth. The tricorner piece of bronze that supports the fork is pierced asymmetrically by a hole that windows the sky. The pitchfork, a basic tool of the Catalan peasant, crowns the work. On the one hand, this element can be seen as a Dada "found object" incorporated into the work, introducing with it an aspect of everyday reality and identifying Miró's Catalan heritage. On the other hand, it can be understood allusively as an image of flight, an arrow, or a bird. Indeed, in many of his other works, both sculptural and graphic, Miró identifies the image of the fork with that of the bird—one of his most frequent poetic images.

Taken together, *Ceramic* and *The Fork* represent two poles of Miró's concerns. One flat and stationary, the other poised as if for flight, these two works provide a perfect counterpoint to each other within the *Labyrinth*.

123

JOAN MIRÓ

Arch

1963
Cement and embedded stones
508 x 615 x 215 cm. (200 x
242⅛ x 84⅝ in.)

In an interview of 1956, Miró discussed the result of his work with Artigas: "I became more and more fascinated [with our sculptures]. Some of them were very big—twelve feet high, nine feet, or four. The large pieces are meant for out-of-doors. I worked in a monumental spirit, thinking of a possible association with architecture. It would be a way of enriching collective architecture."

Six years later Miró realized this ambition with the truly monumental *Arch* that dominates the *Labyrinth*. It is made out of concrete (since no ceramic could be used in sculpture of this scale), and the form is half animal, half architectural. Miró inscribed his personal language of signs in the wet cement, and the surface is given added texture by the stones randomly embedded in it.

The original inspiration for this image probably came from Catalan folk art, in which strangely decorated dolls and beasts that approximate this arch-shape often appear. It is interesting to note that the first time Miró sculpted this shape it was not intended to be an arch. Between 1944 and 1946 he executed a figure entitled *Personage*, made out of terra cotta, standing only fourteen inches high. The only major difference in shape between that piece and the monumental arch is that in the small version a mouthlike opening stretches over the center crossing. Later, in 1962, Miró returned to this image, making a series of bronze maquettes for the *Arch*. As he experimented with the scheme, *Arch* retained its anthropomorphic character: openings like human orifices pierce the surface; undulating forms swell outward here and there; the overall shape suggests some huge legendary beast.

Due to its massive scale, *Arch* takes on a heightened significance akin to that of ceremonial and religious sculpture. In 1939, Miró stated: "If we do not endeavor to discover the religious essence, the magical significance of things, we shall merely add to the sources of stupefaction so freely proffered to man in our day." Seen in this context, *Arch* becomes a mystic portal, an entryway into a magical world.

In this fashion Miró makes concrete the visionary realm seen in his paintings. The emphatic bulk of *Arch* towers over the rest of the *Labyrinth*, but its organic character keeps the work in balance with its natural setting. This is not an arch to march through triumphantly, as were those built for the generals of ancient Rome and the armies of Napoleon. Instead it is a doorway to pass through with awe, as one enters the special reality of Miró.

Musée National Message Biblique
Marc Chagall, Nice

MARC CHAGALL

b. Vitebsk, Russia, 1889

Paradise

Undated
Oil on canvas
185 x 287 cm. (72^{13}/$_{16}$ x 113 in.)

Over a period of more than thirty years, Marc Chagall created a series of paintings, sculptures, and gouaches, which he conceived of as a single work and entitled the *Message Biblique*, or "Message of the Bible." He intended to install this series in a chapel in Vence, but the proposed building was too small to house the vast oeuvre, and it was instead placed in a new museum in Nice, called the Musée National Message Biblique Marc Chagall. The *Message Biblique* includes a large number of preparatory gouaches, a set of large allegorical paintings, a massive stained-glass window, sculptures, and drawings. From the original gouaches, begun in 1931, the artist developed twelve great canvases—the heart of the collection.

Chagall retained the composition of his 1931 gouache *The Creation of Eve*, using it for the entire left half of this painting: in the lower corner is Adam, seated in the lotus position, with his head leaning on his arm in the dreaming pose that Chagall particularly favored. From him, Eve is born, her nakedness covered by a cloud—the impalpable and vague form within which God, according to the Bible, wandered through Paradise.

Immediately after her creation came the temptation of the original couple. Indeed, their temptation stems from her creation. This theme of the fundamental duality of human nature is not a mere vulgar attempt "to explain nature" but is, for Chagall, the essential mystery of life. He was to "stage" his paintings (as one would stage a play), by the poetic means of color and form.

Paradise is that inaccessible universe where man, living in happiness and without time and space, roams in harmony with other creatures, particularly animals, seen everywhere in the painting. In a second painting (not reproduced here), titled *Adam and Eve Driven from Paradise*, Chagall again treated this theme of the harmonious landscape of Paradise, in which man lived in peace with the world and with himself. In contemplating these two canvases, in which the same colorful composition and the same dazzling landscapes appear, one cannot help but think that the highest goal that painting could pursue, or that art itself could have, is to find again, in art—through words, musical notes or colors—this Paradise lost.

From Milton to Chagall, the rich and nostalgic poem of Paradise has taken form again and again, as man explains the origin of his tragic condition in one of the most powerful myths ever created.

MARC CHAGALL

Noah and the Rainbow

Undated
Oil on canvas
205 x 292.5 cm. (80^{11}⁄$_{16}$ x 115^{3}⁄$_{16}$ in.)

At the heart of the Musée Chagall collection is a cycle of twelve large paintings by Marc Chagall, called the *Message Biblique* paintings, in which the two prophets and patriarchs of the Bible are the central figures. Noah is one of the original of these figures in biblical stories—it was he who saved humanity from the Flood and revealed the new, purified world with which God made his covenant. The Bible is rich in these episodes of successive quarrels and reconciliations, symbolized by a dialogue between God and his creatures—in this case Noah, and later, Abraham, Moses, and Jacob. In fact, the cycle of the *Message Biblique* paintings breaks precisely where the direct dialogue between man and God ends, at the moment when the Law is handed down to Moses.

Since this painting is an image of reconciliation, Chagall has composed it on a closed, circular line. The rainbow is one half, and Noah's body is the other.

Two of Chagall's gouaches in the collection are also particularly concerned with this episode, both organized in the form of a perfect circle. This is an image not only of the harmonious tie between man and God, but also of that between the sleeper and his dream; for Chagall allows us to see both the visionary and his vision at the same time.

A second painting forms a kind of companion piece to this one. It is composed of wailing figures with arms lifted to the heavens, flights and disorder. In the distance, a village is burning, symbolic of all wars and persecutions, and in particular of the Holocaust. We see the spectacle of the distress of humanity devouring itself, while Chagall too watches, powerless, over the generations he has depicted. In Chagall's art, man can only escape his miserable and tragic condition in his dreams. And he cannot flee into just any psychic world, but must rise in his dreams into a spiritual world where fantasies take shape and where poetry gives birth to serious, beautiful myths, symbolizing man's perpetual desire to go beyond himself.

129

MARC CHAGALL

Abraham and the Three Angels

Undated
Oil on canvas
190 x 292 cm. (74^{13}⁄$_{16}$ x 115 in.)

This is the only painting with a red background done by Chagall for the *Message Biblique* cycle, and the only one so distinctly influenced by Byzantine and Russian icons. The red background has the effect of making the marvelous wings of the angels stand out toward the viewer, as fragments of pure paint that demonstrate the vibrancy of Chagall's brushstroke. These wings are the descendants in modern art of the Byzantine mosaics, the stained-glass windows of Chartres, or the flowers of Odilon Redon—images of sumptuousness and brilliance that carry a spiritual message and are truly monumental.

Chagall depicted his angels as messengers in action, divine missionaries incarnate in human form. With one shoe on and with one shoe off, the angel in the center of this painting symbolizes the existence of two contrary states within the same creature. This is the meaning one could attribute to the entire painting: in the center, the three angels are bringing to Abraham and Sarah the good news of the birth of a son. In the upper left, they prepare to wreak death on Sodom and Gomorrah. Creation and destruction, life and death, are the center of attention for the painter and for the *Message Biblique*.

131

MARC CHAGALL

The Smiting of the Rock

Undated
Oil on canvas
236 x 232 cm. (93 x 91⅜ in.)

Water is at the center of this story from Exodus: Moses makes it gush forth from the rock to quench the Hebrews' thirst, and thus manifests the divine presence and protection of God. This gift from the Creator springs from a horizon dominated by a reddening sun, symbol of spiritual light.

Chagall has composed this painting with an emphasis on the people rather than on the prophet. He gives us a striking series of portraits, figures of a heterogeneous and touching humanity, moved by a wide spectrum of feelings; many are of children, and some are obviously evocations of the figure of Christ.

This is undoubtedly the most austere painting in the cycle. Over a brown mixture of many tones, Chagall has splashed pure color—a difficult technique which had been tried before by such artists as the Bassani of the Venetian Renaissance, in their landscapes and winterscapes, which were brightened only by the red, yellow, or green costumes of peasants. Eight sketches were done in pastel or oil for this painting alone, and in these one can see how the artist developed and perfected the final version through an increasingly abstract approach to his composition. His greatest concern was with the search for a balance of colors: red and green are here divided into two or three areas, with two bands of yellow at the top and bottom of the painting. Several black circles indicate the positions of the faces, but the drawing itself alters nothing of the colorful composition. On the contrary, it acts like a thread that runs through the structure of the painting and adds to its vibrancy. Regardless of the naive debate over the classification of these works as figurative or nonfigurative, this painting demonstrates the artist's wish to include techniques used by every era of art, and to combine an aesthetic formula, free of representational concerns, with the simplicity of a descriptive story.

132

MARC CHAGALL

The Song of Songs III

Undated
Oil on canvas
149 x 210 cm. (58⅝ x 82¹¹⁄₁₆ in.)

Chagall planned to decorate a room adjoining the Calvary Chapel at Vence with five paintings, smaller than the first twelve of the *Message Biblique* group. For this smaller series of paintings, he chose one theme on which he constructed a series of variations. *The Song of Songs* seemed to him to be the most fitting subject for the central role in his work. This love poem, attributed to King Solomon, is subject to a double interpretation, as both a human and a spiritual text. The dialogue between the Soul and its Creator takes its language from the language of love, and the sensuality of the images sometimes eclipses the "religious" content of the poem.

In his cycle of paintings, Chagall resolutely assumes both interpretations, since he sees love as the fundamental basis of the history of mankind. The love that creates conjures up for us the image of a Demiurge at the beginning of time, and also that of the joined, fertile couple. The five canvases are all painted on a field of reddish pink—the most sensual of colors—and show numerous intertwined couples scattered through heavens crossed by imperious, rhythmic lines.

In the piece reproduced here, the third in the series, Chagall has created a dialogue between pairs of opposites—in this case, man and woman—and has added to it a further dialogue between the two cities of his mental universe: Vitebsk, the absent, the town where he was born, represented in reverse, with its orthodox church, its isbas, and ramparts; and Vence, the present, with its cathedral and high château, as he saw it from his window when he lived there. The image of the one town is like a reflection of the other, but it is an image of a lost reality, which has become a fantasy of the artist, since the towns, as Chagall has painted them, are much more poetic than the actual places. The subject of the painting is, thus, a representation of visions drawn by the artist from his subconscious, and Chagall is placing himself in a long tradition of painters for whom "my only country is the one in my soul."

134

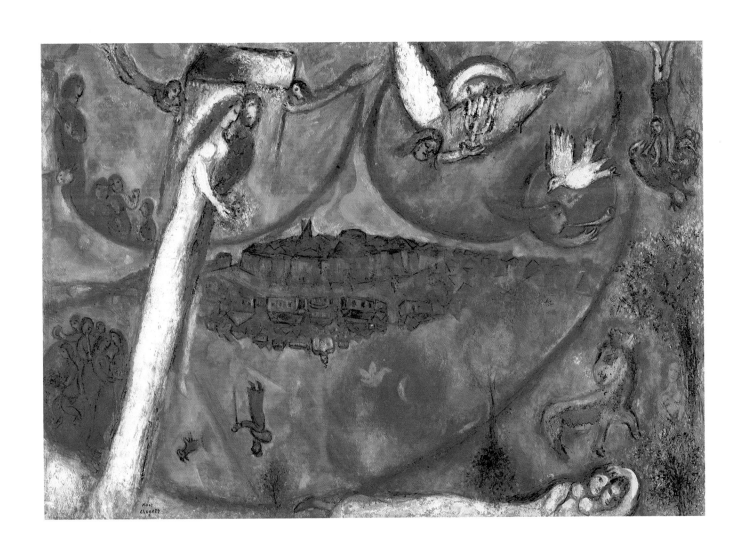

135

MARC CHAGALL

Abraham Prepares to Sacrifice his Son

1931
Oil and gouache
66.5 x 52 cm. (26³⁄₁₆ x 20½ in.)

Chagall based his compositions for the great paintings of the *Message Biblique* on a series of gouaches done earlier. It is thus extremely important to compare the oil paintings of 1954 to 1967 with these earlier gouaches, in order to see the change or lack of change in the artist's intentions. For example, the diagonal, the line used here to indicate the contact between Abraham and the angel grasping his arm, appears again on the arched body of Isaac in a later painting, *The Sacrifice of Isaac.* Chosen for its dynamic character, the diagonal line was a favorite compositional motif of the Baroque painters—the pose of the angel in this painting is similar to that in paintings of Veronese and Rembrandt on the same subject.

In the later version, Chagall was to add the figure of Christ carrying the Cross to the image of Isaac being offered for sacrifice by his father; to a picture that would otherwise be merely illustrative, he added the force of symbol and universal meaning.

Eliezer and Rebecca

1931
Oil and gouache
67 x 52 cm. (26³⁄₁₆ x 20½ in.)

Chagall's gouaches, painted upon his return from Palestine in 1931, are, possibly, a concrete manifestation of the awe the artist felt before the biblical landscape. But it is the power of the artist's technique in these gouaches, and the choice of figures, more than the picturesque evocation of Middle Eastern scenery, that are striking. Chagall, who was scornful of nineteenth-century art, was undoubtedly familiar with the North African and Middle Eastern landscapes of Decamps and Marilhat. However, their style was not for him; this is the only gouache where he allows himself to paint a palm tree and a camel—images he usually considered too academic. It is the colors (particularly the bright red of Rebecca's dress) that best convey the painting's joyful quality—the sense of ascending and dancing—that is so appropriate to the subject: the discovery by Abraham's servant of the wife he will give to Isaac.

136

MARC CHAGALL

Moses

Undated
Stone
53 x 22.9 cm. (20⅞ x 9 in.)

The figure of Moses, at the same time human and awesome, symbolized for Chagall the destiny of humanity, much as did the figure of Christ. These two figures are constantly present in his work, seeming truly to haunt him, and, at the same time, are transposed by him in constantly changing materials and techniques. It is as if he wished to subordinate their deeply symbolic power to a figurative representation and to find in each new medium he used a particular characteristic that would bring out some specific aspect of their significance.

Here, he depicts Moses in stone. The sculpture is carved in the form of a stele, giving the figure both an archaic and a monumental character; it is as much engraved as it is modelled in the round. The figure appears to be part of a bas-relief, of which only the essential details are preserved: Moses, with his eyes closed, bends over the Tablets he has just received, still moved by the contemplation of the divine miracle. All Chagall's characterizations of Moses, whether in ceramic or stone, painted or engraved, drawn or printed, are based on his 1931 preparatory gouaches and on the great finished painting from the *Message Biblique* cycle, entitled *Moses Receiving the Tablets*. This sculpture exemplifies the artist's ever-present wish to create monumental works, to share the qualities of architecture, and to use its materials. The sculpture also demonstrates Chagall's ability to produce works in a variety of media, at the same time that he was painting the *Message Biblique* series—inspired by his previous works and by the Bible itself.

139

MARC CHAGALL

The Creation

1972
Stained glass
465 x 396 cm. (183 x 156 in.;
  The First Four Days)
465 x 266 cm. (183 x 104¾ in.;
  The Fifth and Sixth Days)
465 x 127 cm. (183 x 50 in.;
  The Seventh Day)

When Chagall learned that the French government was going to build the concert hall he wanted for his museum, he decided to create three large windows to decorate and light it. These were not his first stained-glass windows, nor were they his earliest collaboration with Charles Marq and Brigitte Simon, two artists who worked in stained glass. But this was, perhaps, the project that most nearly fulfilled his desire to link visual art closely with music and to give to their relationship the universal religious meaning he sought in all his work.

For these reasons, he chose the theme of the creation of the world for his stained-glass windows. Actually, no other subject could better suit the activity that takes place in this hall: the musician, like the painter, creates a marvelous poetic space, and at that moment mirrors the mythic Creator of the world and the origin of all creation. It is the fulfillment of Chagall's idea of the artist's function.

Against a general background of blues, signifying primal Night gradually dispersed by the rays of the sun, the planets are first revealed, set in motion by a ball of fire thrown by God into the universe. Next, the flowers, animals, and, finally, man appear. *The Creation* is the most refined of the works in the *Message Biblique* cycle. It is made still more effective by the passage of pure light through colored glass, which Chagall and his artisans were able to modulate and disperse in a series of quivering flashes and dominant dark lines created in iron, lead, or grisaille—the black substance that Chagall himself applied to the glass to give the work its meaning and life.

140

141

Musée Matisse, Nice

HENRI MATISSE

b. Le Cateau-Cambrésis, 1869
d. Nice, 1954

Portrait of Mme Matisse

1905
Oil on canvas
46.5 x 38 cm. (18¼ x 15 in.)

This sketch, painted in Collioure in 1905, has an almost symbolic value for the museum, for it introduces into the collection an essential moment in Matisse's work: the decisive visit to Collioure in the summer of 1905, which brought to an end his Divisionist experiments and saw the beginning of Fauvism. This moment was marked historically by the Salon d'Automne of the same year and the Salon des Indépendants the following spring. In addition, this sketch is of particular interest because it was a preparatory study for the *Portrait of Mme Matisse: The Green Line*, in the Copenhagen Statens Museum for Kunst—a veritable manifesto of the Fauve pictorial revolution.

Although this sketch, by its very brief nature, cannot be considered as monumental or as finished a work as the definitive portrait, it nonetheless serves as a preliminary outline for the artist's intentions. We can see here, in its original form, the rigorous analysis and construction of the face created by the brushstrokes and by arbitrary touches of color standing out against the flat backround.

The spirit of the sketch is retained in the Copenhagen *Portrait*; however, by changing the angle of the model's head in the finished painting, Matisse confirmed the power of the image through his use of the famous green stripe which runs vertically down the center of Mme Matisse's face, dominating the chromatic harmony and construction of the painting. This harmonic structure is carefully built by the division of colors, which are broadly flattened or broken up by isolated brushstrokes.

HENRI MATISSE

Storm at Nice

1919–20
Oil on canvas
60 x 73.5 cm. (23⅝ x 28⅞ in.)

Matisse painted the spectacle of a storm during the first of his seasonal sojourns on the Côte d'Azur, a prelude to his eventual move to the Mediterranean sun. His subject here at first appears not to be the "superb and terrifying Midi," but a harmony of greys that are more typical of the northern coast near Etretat. It represents a time when, as Matisse explained in 1919, his palette became severely reduced: "For the moment, I work essentially with a black and grey, with subdued, neutral tones."

The Bay of Angels, a promenade in Nice, often appears in Matisse's works done during his successive stays at the Hôtel Beau-Rivage, and then the Hôtel Méditerranée—both located on the seashore. As was his custom, he studied the different perspectives the view from his balcony offered him. Occasionally a *fête des fleurs* inspired his compositions, but for the most part it was the curve of the seashore that interested him in its relationship to the verticals of the hotel facade.

In contrast to these overhanging views from his balcony, the perspective of *Storm at Nice* is set back from the beach. The force of the storm is shown by a large diagonal that pierces the parallels of the elements of the composition: a minuscule silhouette of a passerby with an umbrella, an embankment awash with rain, a row of blown trees, a howling outraged sea.

At the extreme right of the foreground, the back of a chair (or some other object) has been included on the balcony. It is set at a different angle from the rest of the composition and tends to eliminate the distance between the painter and his subject, while at the same time it expresses his concern in creating a relationship between them.

HENRI MATISSE

HENRI MATISSE

Odalisque with a Red Coffer

1926
Oil on canvas
50 x 64.5 cm. (19⅝ x 25⅜ in.)

During the years 1926–27, Matisse renewed his interest in the Odalisque theme in a series of canvases; the one reproduced here is part of this group. This development is part of a greater concern in his work of this period that focused, around 1925, on the painting *Figure on an Ornamental Background* and the sculpture *Large Seated Nude*.

The *Odalisques* of these years are not presented in terms of the traditional rules of perspective. The paintings' interiors, filled with wall hangings, sofas, and other decorative elements, frame the Odalisques in horizontally layered compositions, with the central band being occupied by the reclining figure. The curtains or wallpaper of these scenes, drawn in strong vertical strokes, constitute a kind of plumb line. This scheme is more or less variable. For example, it is evident in *Odalisque with a Red Coffer* that the quasi-sculptural density of the figure serves as a foil for the interplay of the perpendiculars, whose juxtaposition would otherwise appear abrupt.

In the *Odalisques* that followed, Matisse modified the relationship of the contrasts by his use of furniture and other objects, which are placed at the juncture of the verticals and horizontals in the composition. The series of six *Odalisques*, 1926–27, reproduced in the *Cahiers d'Art* of 1927, illustrates the final evolution of this theme. As in the initial works the sinuousness of the figure punctuates the composition. *Odalisque with a Red Coffer* is also the basis of a lithograph by Matisse.

147

HENRI MATISSE

Two Sketches for "The Dance"

1931–33
Pencil on paper
26.5 x 75 cm. (10$^7/_{16}$ x 29$^1/_2$ in.)

1931–33
Gouache on cut and pasted paper
31 x 77.5 cm. (12$^{13}/_{16}$ x 30$^1/_2$ in.)

The theme of *The Dance* was of interest to Matisse throughout his career; it culminates in two great works: *The Dance* of 1909, painted for the Russian collector Shchukin, and the large decorative mural in the Barnes Foundation.

The museum at Nice does not own any works directly related to the first *Dance*, but a wooden sculpture of three figures forming a ring, called *The Dance*, and a ceramic sculpture, entitled *Danseuse* (also known as *Nymph*), and similar to the wooden sculpture in style, can be linked to *The Dance* of 1909.

The second period of Matisse's art devoted to this theme is associated with *The Dance* of the Barnes Foundation. During his trip to the United States in 1930, Matisse met the art collector Dr. Barnes, who requested that he do a mural for the hall of the Foundation in Merion, Pennsylvania. The subject was to fill three large lunettes which spanned the hall. Matisse began to work on the project at the beginning of 1931 in his atelier on the rue Desiré in Nice. Unfortunately, due to inexact measurements, the composition could not be put in place. This first version of *The Dance* can be found today at the Musée d'Art Moderne de la Ville de Paris. The second version is in place at the Barnes Foundation. The Musée Matisse owns a group of important preparatory studies for these two works, which allows us to follow the development of their compositions. This group includes oil sketches, gouaches, watercolors, and the maquette—reduced in scale—of the final composition in its first version. It is important to note here that it was during the work on *The Dance* that Matisse first used cutout paper painted with gouache.

A series of pencil studies shows the approach he used, revealing the invention needed to adapt the figures to the odd shape of the lunettes. Finally, there are isolated, experimental sketches which study the pose and gesture of the figures. Several among them illustrate the passage from the first version to the second.

149

HENRI MATISSE

Reclining Nude

1935
Charcoal worked with stump on
    paper
37.5 x 56.5 cm. (14¾ x 22¼ in.)

This study of a *Reclining Nude* is one of the milestones in Matisse's work, for it is one of the first sketches that preceded the *Pink Nude* now in the Cone Collection of the Baltimore Museum of Art. This work dominated the artist's career in the 1930s—along with *The Dance*, now in the Barnes Foundation, and his illustrations for Mallarmé's poetry—and is outstanding in its artistic experimentation and technique. Matisse's method in this composition was to work in successive stages, now known only through photographs, erasing and reworking his images. Some stages were modelled in gouache cutouts. This technique appears for the first time in *The Dance*, executed shortly before *Pink Nude*. In both cases, however, it was only a working method, not an end in itself.

The comparison between the drawing reproduced here and the definitive painting allows us to note how Matisse returned to his first idea, while, at the same time, transforming this sensitive and subtle study in charcoal into a linear, abstract figure.

As early as 1906–07, Matisse explored the motif of a reclining nude in some of his greatest works: *Blue Nude*, in the Cone Collection of the Baltimore Museum of Art, a bronze based on the same motif, and a preparatory study for it which is also in the Baltimore Museum. The relationship between these latter works shows an artistic progression similar to the one found in *Pink Nude*.

Inverted Nude with Large Foliage

1936
Charcoal worked with stump on
    paper
33 x 50 cm. (13 x 19⅝ in.)

Matisse's *Inverted Nude with Large Foliage* is a preliminary study for his *Nude Lying on Her Back* (formerly in the Rosenberg Collection). However, the initial pose of the model seen in this drawing was not kept in the final painting. This was a common practice of the artist. He kept very few preparatory sketches in the usual sense of the term, for his experimental studies have their own significance, and can be considered independent works of art. Matisse was particularly predisposed toward the motif of the inverted nude, which inspired a series of brilliant pen-and-ink studies, done in 1935–36.

In all his drawings, he utilized the possibilities of the graphic media in all their range and subtlety. Around the figure of the inverted nude, the modelled shadows bring a variety of decorative elements into play with great brio. In contrast, the charcoal lines present a purified version of the motif. It dominates the other elements, bringing attention back to the figure. The leaves, worked with the stump, create a shadowed area which gives emphasis to the curves and volume of the nude.

150

151

HENRI MATISSE

Nymph in the Forest, "Greenery"

1936–42
Oil on canvas
234 x 191 cm. (92⅛ x 75³⁄₁₆ in.)

In the 1930s, Matisse returned to the theme of the nude in the landscape, which he had used often in the period from 1904 to 1910, from *Luxe, Calme et Volupté* to *The Dance* and *Music*. In 1932, he took up, among other bucolic themes (such as those in his illustrations of Mallarmé's poetry) the motif of the nymph and the faun, which first appeared in his work in 1907, in the central panel of a ceramic triptych now in the Karl-Osthaus Museum in Hagen. After that time, this theme often reappeared in his work. He began to use it in his drawing in May 1935, while working on a landscape inspired by his illustrations of Mallarmé, and Des Esseintes. He decided to include the nymph and faun theme in his landscape, which he then called *"Greenery."*

The painting, now known as *Nymph in the Forest*, was exhibited at the Paul Rosenberg gallery in 1936. A contemporary photograph shows it framed with a border decorated in the spirit of his tapestry *Tahitian Window*, also first exhibited at that time. The similarity between the two works suggests that the *Nymph in the Forest* might have been intended as a sketch for a tapestry.

Matisse was again working on *"Greenery"* when a series of photographs was taken in December 1940 by Varian Fry in his Regina studio; the painting still had its decorated frame, and the canvas still bore the trace of the studies and alterations it had undergone over the previous years. The landscape is crossed by strong, almost abstract vertical lines, made concrete as tree trunks; a stream creates the illusion of depth by cutting their monumental rhythm with its diagonal line. By introducing the nymph and faun into his composition, Matisse completed the balance of the painting, at the same time reinforcing the illusion of depth by including the extended figure, who traces a horizontal line on the ground.

The famous *Pink Nude* of 1935, in the Cone Collection of the Baltimore Museum of Art, was the culmination of an exceptional series of works (see the commentary on the *Reclining Nude*, 1935, page 150). With *Nymph in the Forest*, Matisse concluded his studies on this theme of the reclining nude, giving it a broader dimension and meaning through his evocation of the original harmony of nature.

HENRI MATISSE

Still Life with Pomegranates

1947–48
Oil on canvas
81 x 60.5 cm. (31⅞ x 23¾ in.)

Still Life with Pomegranates is one in a series of Vence *Interiors*, of 1947–48. An issue of *Verve* published this group of paintings in 1948; with a few exceptions, they are the last of Matisse's easel paintings. In concluding this aspect of his art, he used one of his favorite themes, that of the window. As in other versions of this motif, in the Vence *Interiors* the window is seen from inside a room. The *Interiors*, with their dazzling color, demonstrate all the richness of the artist's vision by showing the many facets of this theme.

Still Life with Pomegranates has a universal character and a significance that goes beyond the personal experience of the artist. It represents the highest level of his achievement in his synthesis of the art of the colorist with the exacting requirements of the designer.

Under the restrictive title of *Still Life*, Matisse brings together several themes which unwind in the successive planes of the picture: the still life in the foreground and the interior of which it is a part; the window looking out on the exterior; and the open air represented by the palm tree spreading out against the sky. In a 1942 radio interview, Matisse explained: "In my mind, space is one—from the horizon to the interior of my studio." He connects these elements in a unique world, integrating them in a rigorous composition, based on a rich chromatic harmony. A deep black is interposed between vibrant and intense tones, supplying the unity and cohesion which conserves the bright autonomy of each of the colors. "It is by these blacks that I exist," Matisse said to Renoir, insisting on the importance of the diverse roles that black played in his painting. This role is evident if one compares this picture to another *Still Life with Pomegranates*. That version is very like the one reproduced here except that Matisse chose to use Venetian red instead of black. In order to equalize the force of this brilliant color, the artist adjusted the details of the composition, conferring greater importance on the table and fruit in the foreground.

HENRI MATISSE

La Serpentine

1909
Bronze
56.5 cm. high (22¼ in.)

Reclining Nude III

Ca. 1929
Bronze
28.5 cm. high (11¼ in.)

When the Jean Matisse Donation, given to the State by Mme Jean Matisse, was installed in the museum at Nice in June 1979, the sculpted works of Matisse became a large part of the collection. The museum thus became one of the few places where one can find original casts of almost all of Matisse's sculptures on permanent exhibition. Ranging from monumental figures to infinitely small ones, this is a collection of great variety, in which Matisse explored a new dimension of form and experimented with diverse techniques. In some of the sculptures a smooth, polished modelling amplifies the volume of the figure; in others, the form is crushed by an abrupt découpage of planes and volumes.

These bronzes consist of both portraits and nudes. Matisse subjected each piece to a rigorous analysis, manipulating the medium of bronze to its fullest advantage. Throughout his career, from 1903 to 1950, the poses of Matisse's sculptures developed and unfolded. One can find versions of his nudes in standing, seated, crouching, and reclining positions, sometimes alone and sometimes in group compositions. One of his most powerful early works is *La Serpentine*, of 1909. This standing figure takes on the fluid pose suggested by her name.

Reclining Nude III, one in a series of works on this theme, repeats the twisted form of *La Serpentine* in an entirely new context. Executed in 1927, it displays a much blockier conception of the figure, monumentalizing it despite its small scale.

156

157

HENRI MATISSE

The Slave

1900–03
Bronze
92 cm. high (36¼ in.)

The Musée Matisse originally owned four sculptures by Matisse, all of which are of high quality. Among these was *The Slave*, the first major sculpture by the artist. It was executed between 1900 and 1903, and is one of his rare masculine nudes.

Auguste Rodin (see page 179) was the leading sculptor in Paris at that time. His sculptures had won him both critical and popular acclaim. Matisse himself was deeply impressed by Rodin's achievement and bought the plaster model of Rodin's portrait of Rochefort from Ambroise Vollard in 1899. While *The Slave* is in no way a repetition of Rodin's work, it emulates that master's bold and expressive style. Indeed, Matisse studied sculpture under one of Rodin's pupils, Antoine Bourdelle, working with him for several months in 1900. The modelling of *The Slave* emphasizes the aggresive stance and bold musculature of the figure. Matisse painted a number of oil studies in preparation for this work. The first bronze version was cast in 1908 and was exhibited that year at the Salon d'Automne.

158

159

HENRI MATISSE

Blue Nude IV

1952
Gouache on cut and pasted paper
102.9 x 76.8 cm. (40½ x 30½ in.)

The *Blue Nude* shown here belongs to a series of four figures done in gouache cutout. It was begun first, but finished after the other three, hence its title, *Blue Nude IV*. This series, along with a notebook of studies, marks his departure on a new path of art.

Blue Nude IV is the last in a long series of images of crouching nudes. The motif appears very early in the work of the artist, notably in his *Joie de Vivre*, 1905–06, now in the Barnes Foundation. Among the many variations on the pose, his most original interpretation is that of the figures in pyramidal compositions. In these, Matisse drew a seated figure on the ground, building the composition upward from the curvilinear bend of one of the folded legs of the model, to the arabesque of the folded arms which balance out the figure. It is not surprising that this theme, suggesting a form cramped in space, was most completely expressed in sculpture and, eventually, in the gouache cutouts. In many respects the *Blue Nudes* are a remarkable departure from Matisse's earlier style.

The landmark painting *Decorative Figure on an Ornamental Background* of 1925, now in the Musée National d'Art Moderne in Paris, brought monumentality to the nude motif in Matisse's painting. However, in the very technique and concept in which it was painted, the figure was intimately linked to its decorative surroundings, which Matisse used to suggest the triangular ground on which the figure rests.

In contrast, Matisse has freed his *Blue Nudes* from their surroundings. Here, his technique of modelling white space is the reverse of his pen-and-ink style, in which contour lines created forms by encompassing and defining areas of white. It is the area outside the figure that creates space and volume, communicating a third and sculptural dimension to the *Blue Nudes*. Through these figures, Matisse approaches the problem of form in a new manner, and introduces us to a new aspect of his art—a concept of form that enlivens many of his last great works.

H MATISSE 52

161

HENRI MATISSE

Study for a Chasuble

1949–51
Gouache on cut and pasted paper
130 x 200 cm. (51 ³⁄₁₆ x 78 ¾ in.)

The Dominican chapel in Vence, decorated by Matisse, has been written about both by experts on the artist and by many other authors of diverse interests. It has prompted many questions, since it introduces, late in his career, a subject that was apparently foreign to the themes that had occupied him formerly. Matisse himself acknowledged this change of interest in a letter of June 1951 to Monseigneur Rémond, Bishop of Nice: "This work required four years of exclusive and assiduous concentration and it is the end result of my active life. Despite its imperfections, I consider it my masterpiece."

Matisse had moved to Vence during the Second World War. His house, a villa named *Le Rêve*, was located near an abbey of Dominican nuns, one of whom, Sister Jacques, was his nurse in Nice. She told him of her desire to see her convent renovated. The project appealed to Matisse, and with Brother Rayssiguier, he began to consider how it might be done.

One of the unique aspects of this project is that Matisse undertook to redesign not only the architectural elements of the chapel, but all the vestments, apparel, and other objects of religious ceremony. Illustrated here is a study for the chasubles that Matisse designed. He used his usual symbols and technique of this period—gouache cutouts in vibrant colors—but invests the work with spiritual significance.

HENRI MATISSE

Two Studies for Stained-glass Windows

1949–51
Stained glass
60 x 90 cm. (23⅝ x 35⁷⁄₁₆ in.)

1949–51
Stained glass
76 x 90 cm. (29⁵⁄₁₆ x 35⁷⁄₁₆ in.)

After painting the *Dance* mural for the Barnes Foundation (see p. 149), Matisse wished to continue to decorate walls and other large surfaces. The Dominican chapel in Vence offered such an opportunity: here he could unite all the arts together. Not only did he adapt his style to architecture, but he conceived of a functional whole as well—an interior decor with an assortment of furnishings done in different techniques. A major part of this scheme is a set of stained-glass windows.

These windows are a further development of his mural art, for they introduce luminosity into his work. The chapel has no actual murals; instead, these windows filter the light as it enters the interior, and are, themselves, brilliant essays in color. Reproduced here are two of his studies for these windows, executed in glass. As he had with the vestments for the chapel, Matisse has used his familiar vocabulary of bold, simple forms.

The study of his preparatory works permits us to understand the painter and his art. Indeed, knowledge of these works is necessary to a full enjoyment of the chapel itself. A visit to Vence shows us the richness of Matisse's art, but a more significant survey of his career is to be found in the Musée Matisse in Nice. Here it is possible to appreciate the full range of this artist's remarkable achievement.

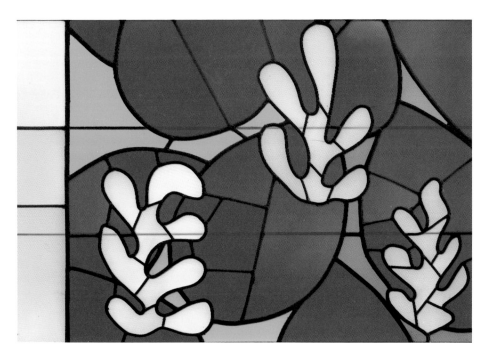

165

Musée des Beaux-Arts Jules Chéret, Nice

JULES CHERET

b. Paris, 1836
d. Nice, 1932

Portrait of Arlette Dorgère

1904
Pastel, 109 x 62 cm. (42$^7_8$ x
24$^3/_8$ in.)

Jules Chéret, the *Belle Epoque* artist and acknowledged inventor of the poster, began his career as a lithographer in a printing house in Paris, and only later was admitted to the Ecole Nationale de Dessin. Unable to support himself as an artist in Paris, he went to London, where he spent ten years. His first major commission there was the design for a poster for Offenbach's *Orpheus in Hell*, but it was an isolated one. Eventually he returned to Paris and, having obtained financial support from the perfumer Rimmel, founded a lithographic workshop. In 1866 he produced his first colored lithograph. This activity flourished, and as he became known and sought as a poster artist, he was able to devote some time to painting as well. Although he was made famous by his posters, his great talent also procured him numerous official and private commissions for paintings and decorations, among them, murals for Baron Joseph Vitta and Maurice Fenaille, and for the Hôtel de Ville in Paris and the Préfecture of Nice. As well as these large projects, he made a great number of pastels and drawings, many of them portraits. He was a master of the drawn line and above all a virtuoso illustrator of glorious and cheerful femininity. The critic and historian of turn-of-the-century art Camille Mauclair accurately remarked that his women are animated dolls who think of nothing, but give one something to think about.

A friend of the Impressionists, principally of Monet, Chéret knew how to avoid the stumbling blocks of academicism and the passing fads of the period, and yet, at the same time, was a recorder *par excellence* of his era. His alchemy of color makes his work a veritable fireworks display.

In his late years he was struck by blindness but, already a rich man, Chéret lived to the age of ninety-six in the Villa Floréal on the slopes of Mount Boron near Nice.

Mauclair said: "These posters brought a note of art to a field which was formerly nonexistent. Paris was enchanted. They saw their walls sing. Soon the central figure became famous—this petite blonde woman with the upturned nose, dancing in a short skirt, who seemed to shout her joy in a world of Pierrots and Harlequins. The 'Chérette' was born, she became the model for Parisian women." This portrait of a woman, in pastel, perfectly exemplifies Chéret's "petite blonde."

166

CARLE VANLOO

b. Nice, 1705
d. Paris, 1765

Neptune and Amymone

1757
Oil on canvas
320 x 320 cm. (126^{5}/$_{16}$ x 126^{5}/$_{16}$ in.)

Carle Vanloo, born in 1705 in Nice but of Dutch origin, was a member of a group of painters of the French School who worked throughout Europe during the seventeenth and eighteenth centuries. This canvas and three others by Boucher, Pierre, and Vien were done as studies for a tapestry called the *Amours des Dieux*, given in 1757 by Louis XV to the Marquis of Marigny as a gift from the King to his Director of Royal Buildings. The subject is drawn from the work of the mythologist Hygin. Amymone, one of the fifty daughters of Danaos, is pursued by a satyr; saved by the sea god Neptune, she succumbs to him in gratitude. The three other couples chosen to illustrate the theme of the loves of the gods were more familiar subjects in the history of painting: Boucher's *Venus and Vulcan* (now in the Louvre); the *Rape of Europe* by Pierre (in Arras, the Musée des Beaux-Arts); and *Pluto and Persephone* by J.M. Vien (in Grenoble, Musée des Beaux-Arts). There is a sketch of this canvas in a collection in Paris, a sketch that is more alive and more narrative than the final work. In the completed painting, the composition is made more static in order to emphasize the couple standing side by side, monumental against the background of an empty sky.

Carle was very well known in his time, as he was the court painter of Louis XV, and the Director of the Royal Academy; his work included a broad range of topics: portraits, genre paintings, and religious and mythological scenes.

An examination of this painting reveals an interesting symbolic theme. The left part of the canvas, a large space which is relatively empty, is occupied by tritons and sea horses, the traditional cortège of the god of the seas. In contrast, the right side, containing a dense forest and the satyr, is placed under the protection of Earth with its fertile, procreative power. The union of Amymone, a terrestrial divinity, and Neptune, the sea god, is due to the power of Love. It is a symbolic union (almost alchemical) of the complementary elements, Earth and Water. There are analogous erotic themes in Veronese's canvas *Mars and Venus United by Love*, at the Metropolitan Museum in New York.

168

169

JEAN HONORE FRAGONARD

b. Grasse, 1732
d. Paris, 1806

Head of an Old Man

Ca. 1765
Oil on canvas
60 x 50 cm. (23$^5/_8$ x 19$^{11}/_{16}$ in.)

Although when young he was an assistant notary by profession, Fragonard's true interest was always in painting. He entered the atelier of François Boucher, who placed him under the direction of Chardin, and by 1752 he had been awarded the Grand Prix de Rome. An anecdote has it that Boucher made this prophetic remark: "You leave for Italy, my boy. If you study Michelangelo and Raphael, you are . . . lost." The pupil followed the advice of his master, rejecting the classicism of Rome. He forsook the official commissions and large decorative projects, preferring more intimate compositions in which his imagination created a world of theater and dreams. He, even more than Boucher, incarnated all the subtle charm of the French eighteenth century. The revolution of 1789 was a terrible blow to Fragonard; it destroyed the courtly world of the Rococo which had given him a major part of his inspiration. In this portrait, Fragonard demonstrates his admiration for the Dutch painting of the seventeenth century—in particular, for the mature works of Hals and Rembrandt. The range of color and the rich mixtures of paint are very much like those of the Master of the *Night Watch*. The pigment is wonderfully well preserved, as the painting was executed *alla prima* (without interruption), an important factor contributing to the durability of the work.

This masterpiece clearly shows that Fragonard, known primarily as a master of pictorial eroticism, could become meditative in representing old age. (It is, perhaps, a symbolic representation, for we cannot be sure that it is drawn from a model.) Goethe said of old age that it consists in gradually drawing oneself back from appearances. Here, the intensity of the figure's look seems to illuminate and dominate the flesh, which is drawn back from the face.

171

JEAN BAPTISTE CARPEAUX

b. Valenciennes, 1827
d. Courbevoie, 1875

The Three Graces

1874
Polished plaster
75 cm. high (29½ in.)

Jean Baptiste Carpeaux, the son of a laborer, became the official sculptor of the Second Empire in spite of the fact that he was the very opposite of an academician. He refused to work in a detailed manner, and was the enemy of the "finished work"; he prized spontaneity and was one of the prophets of modern sculpture—sculpture founded on the struggle to unite the soul of the artist with the very material that he tries to overcome. This student of "roughness" prepared the path for Rodin, who owes him much.

This sculptural group reiterates the classical theme of the Three Graces, so popular in the eighteenth century, without mimicking the classical style. It is a variation on a sculpture entitled *Dance*, done for the facade of the Paris Opera. On August 17, 1865, Carpeaux had received a commission for a group of three figures to decorate the new Opera. The architect, Garnier, chose four themes: *Harmony, Music, Lyric Drama*, and *Dance*. Carpeaux was commissioned to execute a sculpture of this last. He first presented maquettes for *Drama* and *Comedy*, which Garnier rejected. The intention of this sculpture is to express motion; in it, a group of maidens is posed around an invisible, inspirational spirit. In the version for the opera, now in the Louvre, this spirit is personified in a fourth, central figure.

Carpeaux spent two years on studies before completing his maquette; the time and labor taken to achieve it impoverished him, and when it finally appeared, the work caused a scandal. The order from above was to execute another *Dance* to be "treated with decency and conforming to the aspirations of the public." Only the approach of the Prussians saved Carpeaux's work.

172

173

PAUL DESIRE TROUILLEBERT

b. Paris, 1829
d. Paris, 1900

The Servant of the Harem

1874
Oil on canvas
130 x 97 cm. (51$\frac{5}{16}$ x 38$\frac{3}{16}$ in.)

"In the nineteenth century, a trip to Algiers became for painters as indispensable as a pilgrimage to Italy. They went to learn from the sun, to study the light, to look for native types, primitive customs, and exotic scenes. Utilitarians may say that Algeria was useless, contributing nothing to France. But those of us who are not economists love her, for she furnished us with her soul, inspiring a new element in French art." It was thus that the great nineteenth-century art critic Théophile Gautier paid homage to the Oriental atmosphere in *L'Abécédaire du Salon de 1861*.

This influence was present in Europe as early as the eighteenth century and can be clearly seen in some of the paintings of Boucher, in *The Persian Letters* of Montesquieu, and in the *Abduction from the Seraglio* by Mozart. By the nineteenth century a taste for the Oriental pervaded the cultural atmosphere of Europe, affecting all artists, from Ingres to Delacroix and even to Manet, inspiring much in the Romantic movement. It was a fascination with another world, a world entirely foreign but bound to Europe. This was a false image, for at its heart was an occidental fantasy. "Our view of the Orient is always thus; it is a world too distant from ours and therefore beyond our grasp. A political event—the Greek revolt [against the Turks in 1821]—put it in fashion. Another western political event—the conquest of Algeria—prolonged it. But will this taste endure?" wrote the critic Castagnary, about the Salon of 1869.

Trouillebert is certainly not a great master, but his *Servant of the Harem* is an incontestable success. A foreign eroticism, seductive anatomical disproportions, a sure technique, and a highly symbolic date—1874, the year of the first exhibition of a group of painters calling themselves the Impressionists—all contribute to our continuing fascination with this painting.

174

175

ALEXANDER CABANEL

b. Montpelier, 1824
d. Paris, 1888

Tamar

1875
Oil on canvas
180 x 248 cm. (70$^7/_8$ x 97$^5/_8$ in.)

This painting is a highly academic biblical illustration from the second book of Samuel:

> And it came to pass after this, that Absalom the son of David had a fair sister, whose name was Tamar; and Amnon the son of David loved her. And Amnon was so vexed, that he fell sick for his sister Tamar; for she was a virgin; and Amnon thought it hard for him to do anything to her. . . . Howbeit he would not harken unto her voice: but, being stronger than she, forced her, and lay with her. Then Amnon hated her exceedingly; so that the hatred wherewith he hated her was greater than the love wherewith he had loved her. And Amnon said unto her, Arise, be gone. . . . And Tamar put ashes on her head, and rent her garment of divers colors that was on her, and laid her hand on her head, and went on crying. . . . But when king David heard of all these things, he was very wroth. And Absalom spake unto his brother Amnon neither good nor bad: for Absalom hated Amnon, because he had forced his sister Tamar.

It represents the taste of the Academy at this period, when the Impressionists were first causing scandals among the members of the Salon. Alexander Cabanel was the *Cher Maître* of the Second Empire: Member of the Institute, Professor at the Ecole des Beaux-Arts, *Commandeur* of the Legion of Honor—and today unknown. The advent of Impressionism eclipsed his seemingly immortal "monuments."

In the *Gazette des Beaux-Arts* of 1880, Philippe de Chennevières perfectly expressed the good opinion of the critics and Salon officials of Cabanel's own time:

> Cabanel today holds for us the venerable place that Carle Vanloo, the court painter of Louis XV, filled during that other century: the same soft and harmonious charm of the palette is evident, the same science of draftsmanship—flowing and correct—a composition wisely put together.

AUGUSTE RODIN

b. Paris, 1840
d. Meudon, 1917

The Age of Bronze

1877
Bronze
189 cm. high (74$^7/_{16}$ in.)

Rodin, rejected by the Salon of 1864 because his work was too naturalistic, went to Belgium, where he worked for a few years and then produced his first great sculpture, *The Age of Bronze*, whose plaster cast he exhibited in the Salon of 1877. It is a free study modelled on the figure of Rodin's friend Auguste Neyt, a Belgian soldier who posed for the sculpture. The sculpture affirms his total originality and his deep opposition to the then popular academicism. Some of the Salon's official sculptors, however, accused him of having taken a cast directly from nature. The authenticity of Rodin's work was defended by a group of colleagues known for their intellectual integrity. Among them were Chapu, Paul Dubois, Carrier-Belleuse, and his old teacher Falguière. Also titled *Man Awakening with Nature*, or *Man Defeated*, *The Age of Bronze* represents more than a year's effort in the life of the sculptor. If the theme of this work seems too familiar, and relatively uninspired—man at his spiritual birth, or man in his primitive state—still, the sculpture is free of all trite narrative and reflects an idea in art which goes back centuries. It evokes the tension of the *Slaves* of Michelangelo: man as neither angel nor beast, but born of animality. Here the effect of Darwinism on the art of the late nineteenth century can be seen. But in Rodin's spiritual vision, man also, strives toward an absolute, which urges him on and which he does not understand.

179

ALFRED SISLEY

b. Paris, 1839
d. Moret-sur-Loing, 1899

Path on the Water's Edge

1880
Oil on canvas
55 x 70 cm. (21⅝ x 27⁹⁄₁₆ in.)

Alfred Sisley was of British nationality, but spent most of his life in France, and never obtained the French citizenship he so desired. In 1862 he was a student at the Ecole des Beaux-Arts atelier of the artist Charles Gleyre. There he met Monet, Renoir, and Bazille, with whom he formed a lasting friendship. The instruction of Gleyre had little influence on him; he preferred to study the work of Corot, Théodore Rousseau, Courbet, and Daubigny—the Barbizon painters. He participated in several of the Impressionist exhibitions, including the scandalous first one, of 1874. Durand-Ruel, the Impressionists' dealer, gave him a one-man exhibition in 1883. He died in the poorest of circumstances, never knowing the great enthusiasm for his art that came, ironically, a short time after his death.

Sisley's art, lyrical, modest, and frank, had been overshadowed by the prophetic genius of Monet. In fact, no other artist than Sisley could better translate into paint the landscapes of the Ile-de-France.

In this canvas, Sisley beautifully interprets the sunset on the water's edge at the exact time of evening when a light fog rises to meet the fleecy afternoon clouds.

181

FELIX ZIEM

b. Beaune, 1821
d. Paris, 1911

Study of Flags

Ca. 1895
Oil on panel
27 x 42 cm. ($10^5/_8$ x $16^1/_2$ in.)

Ziem was of Croatian origin on his father's side and of French Burgundian descent on his mother's. His first works of art were in architecture, but he quickly became fascinated by watercolor and inspired by the landscapes he saw during his travels through Russia, the Côte d'Azur, Turkey, and Italy. It was primarily Venice, however—that receptacle of all the fantasy of the West and East—which conquered him. Like many artists before him, Ziem painted numerous *vedute*, or "views" of the city; in these, the sunsets of Claude Lorrain are joined with the exaltation of Canaletto and the nostalgia of Guardi. The quality of his work has often been overlooked because of his enormous productivity, but his spontaneity, the freedom of his brushstrokes and colors, make him a little-known gem—only recently rediscovered—of the French landscape school of the late nineteenth century.

But Ziem's art, after a first examination, is quite distant from the spirit of the Impressionists. It is true that, like theirs, his art is alive with the spirit of nature. His many landscapes, which look as though they might have been painted outside, in the open air, are similar on the surface to the Impressionists' *plein-air* landscapes. But Ziem, following the classical approach and quite contrary to the Impressionists' principles, worked inside, in a studio. (Let us not forget that Monet, in his late *Water Lilies*, did the same thing.) In any case, Ziem's best works, as exemplified by this study, anticipate the lyrical abstraction of the 1940s and the Action Painting of Jackson Pollock—a creative anticipation that parallels that of Monet in his most abstract works.

GUSTAV ADOLF MOSSA

b. Nice, 1883
d. Nice, 1971

The Satiated Siren

1905
Oil on canvas
81 x 54 cm. (31⁷/₈ x 21¹/₄ in.)

David and Bathsheba

1906
Oil on canvas
80 x 65 cm. (31¹/₂ x 25⁹/₁₆ in.)

184

The iconography of this Symbolist painting refers explicitly to the ancient myth of the Sirens, who, according to tradition, were birds with the faces of women. By the sweetness of their song, they lured mariners to the rocks where they lived, only to make them founder on the reefs, and then to devour them.

In this painting, Gustav Adolf Mossa, a native of Nice and one of the most interesting representatives of Symbolism, has suggested a specific connection between the city of Nice and the Sirens. It is interesting to note that he has shown Nice engulfed by a flood, recalling the great deluges of myths, and dominated by the Siren, who is satiated by human flesh. In the background, the inundated monuments of Nice—some still in existence today—can be seen: the Church of Nôtre Dame, the railroad station, and the monument commemorating the incorporation of Nice into France.

Because of Mossa's painterly aggressiveness, this work of art anticipates the statements of Superrealism. By its audacity, its derision of the symbol of the *femme fatale*, and its profanation of the iconic images of art—all of which baffled his contemporaries—this painting is typical of Mossa and of the qualities that make a Mossa exhibition unforgettable.

In 1906, Mossa's art became more calm, after the nervous explosion of 1905, visible in *The Satiated Siren. David and Bathsheba* marks his return to his more usual artistic sources—those of Italy and Art Nouveau.

The Italian references in this painting are numerous: the Florentine armor of Uriah, towers recalling those of Pavia copied by Mossa in 1903, the small vase on the balustrade—an allusion to Carpaccio—the foreshortening of the horse inspired by Uccello, and the medal-like profile from Pisanello. The influence of Art Nouveau is also present—Bathsheba is dressed in the fashion of 1906, the border of David's cape evokes the style of Benedictus, and the style of the collar of the greyhound is northern Art Nouveau. As is often the case with Mossa, the work is constructed like a collage. The modelled profile of David emerges as a two-dimensional decorative mass. The left hand of Bathsheba, which one guesses was wandering under David's cape, is completely disjointed and looks like an object that defies anatomy. Uriah's horse shows a horseshoe completely turned around to indicate a gallop. Mossa is not concerned with verisimilitude; rather, his means of expression is to juxtapose elements of reality chosen for their visual harmony, so that a unity is often achieved in the painting in defiance of their logical connection.

From the sheer terror of his subject matter of 1905, Mossa has moved to the expression of a perversity resulting from a more subtle evil: the interrelation of the false innocence of the consenting Bathsheba and the concupiscence of David.

PIERRE AUGUSTE RENOIR

b. Limoges, 1841
d. Cagnes, 1919

Les Grandes Baigneuses

Ca. 1903–05
Oil on canvas
133 x 166 cm. (52³/₈ x 65³/₈ in.)

Renoir painted a number of variants of his famous *Bathers*. *Les Grandes Baigneuses* of Nice constitutes a version of the *Baigneuses* in the Tyson Collection of the Philadelphia Museum of Art. The most complete rendition is found in the Louvre. He began the Philadelphia work after his return from Italy in 1882, finished it in 1885, and exhibited it two years later. It was inspired by a bas-relief by Girardon at Versailles and had numerous preparatory drawings. It clearly shows Renoir's experiments in the simplification of volume and the purity of line in the style of Raphael and Ingres. The Nice version, seen here, was done about 1903–05; although the theme and the structure seem identical to the Philadelphia example, the treatment is no longer that of the Ingresque period. The light rubbings allow us to see the extraordinary preparatory pencilling, left unfinished either by accident or by design, from which comes the reciprocal play between the insubstantial and the solid forms. This is the secret of Renoir's finest achievements, and is based on the voluptuousness of the pictorial technique.

During this period Renoir had rheumatism, and fell in love with the Mediterranean regions; in 1903 he settled in Cagnes. It was there that, overcoming his physical pain, he began to capture the sumptuous natural light of the Midi, rediscovering the innocence of Greek Paganism. Some years earlier, Nietzsche too had discerned in this Niçois region that Arcadian reality over which Dionysos reigned.

187

KEES VAN DONGEN

b. Delfshaven, 1877
d. Monte Carlo, 1968

Portrait of the Haitian Ambassador Casseus

Ca. 1920
Oil on canvas
212 x 132 cm. ($83^7/_{16}$ x $51^{15}/_{16}$ in.)

Born in Holland in 1877, Kees van Dongen settled at the age of twenty in Paris, where he breathed in the vibrant atmosphere of the bohemian life of Montmartre. He was one of the most violent of the Fauves, and his paintings of the beginning of the century are an essential link between the French Fauvist movement and the German Expressionism of the avant-garde groups of Dresden. Van Dongen exhibited both with the Fauves and with the German group Die Brücke.

After the end of World War I, Van Dongen became the most famous of the worldly portraitists who recorded the Roaring Twenties. He had a rare faculty for the art of the portrait, and was able to flatter the external aspect of the model while at the same time revealing the subject's internal hollowness. Exploring beneath false appearances, he brought the weaknesses of his sitters to life; it was the critical vision of a moralist, but that did not prevent a frivolous society from celebrating the painter and applauding his audacity.

Among the subjects immortalized by Van Dongen were Anatole France, Arletty, and Maurice Chevalier. Casseus, the ambassador to Paris from Haiti, mingled in cafe society—the diverse and astonishing fauna of *tout Paris*. Here, the subject seems a bit less complacent than are Van Dongen's portraits of women: sophistication has become a vigorous elegance. The little black porter on the left evokes the hieratic images of the servants in Egyptian tomb art. The painting becomes a nocturnal symphony crossed by the golden burst of the embroidery of the uniform; it is a vivid presence which subtly fades into shadow.

189

RAOUL DUFY

b. Le Havre, 1877
d. Forcalquier, 1953

**The Casino of the Jetée-
    Promenade with Two
    Caleches, Nice**

1927
Oil on canvas
38 x 45 cm. (14^{15}/$_{16}$ x 17^{11}/$_{16}$ in.)

Born in Le Havre in 1877, Raoul Dufy was influenced by his contact with the Impressionists and was familiar with the radical experiments of the Fauves and Cubists. But it was in Vence during the years 1919 to 1922 that he defined his own style, based on juxtaposed and broken lines and a strong sense of narrative, with images drawn on a uniformly colored ground.

This canvas immortalizes one of the most important buildings in the city of Nice during the *Belle Epoque*—a building that fascinated Dufy throughout his career: the Casino on the Jetée-Promenade. Inspired by the British bathing jetties, the first Jetée-Promenade burned down in 1883 just before its inauguration. Redesigned and rebuilt, it opened in 1891. Containing cafes, a theater, restaurants, and gaming rooms, the Jetée immediately became one of the centers of the social scene in Nice. This strange Byzantine-Moorish building was demolished in 1944. While one side faced the sea, the other fronted on the Promenade des Anglais, which runs along the Bay of Angels, the most elegant thoroughfare in Nice, and a boulevard known throughout the world. At first a mere path, the promenade was built in 1823, and soon became one of the most popular sites for the many painters who frequented the Côte d'Azur.

191

LEOPOLD SURVAGE

b. Moscow, 1879
d. Paris, 1968

Desire

1928
Oil on canvas
400 x 200 cm. (157$\frac{1}{2}$ x 78$\frac{3}{4}$ in.)

Léopold Survage, born in Russia, discovered modern western art through the works in the great Shchukin Collection in Moscow and was especially influenced by the famous Matisse paintings that he saw there. When he moved to Paris in 1908, he discovered Cézanne, and eventually became one of the painters to develop the style called Synthetic Cubism. He had shown his work with the Cubists in 1911, and just before World War I he worked on a film entitled *Rhythmes Colorés*, intended to be animated abstract drawings. For it, he produced some 200 totally abstract studies; these went beyond the merely nonobjective and were a forerunner of cinematic art, placing Survage among the initiators of abstraction. The experiments of Robert Delaunay, done at about the same time, pursued a parallel course.

Survage combined the rigorous geometrization of Cézanne with the arabesques and flattened colors of Matisse in his highly plastic art. The discovery of the light of the Midi had caused generations of artists at the end of the nineteenth and the beginning of the twentieth century to alter their art. Some early works by Survage had been done in Nice and Villefranche-sur-Mer. As Matisse had done, this artist, whose first influences had been in the cold north, now discovered that landscape and light and brought its remarkable luminosity to his work. The fullness and monumentality of this composition of 1928 are similar to some contemporary ideas of Picasso, particularly Picasso's reinterpretation of Neoclassicism. The Cubism of the period after the First World War showed a desire for a clear return to order; a strong concern for order and structure was visible in the work of most of the champions of modern art, who were enjoying a well-earned rest while they gathered new energies. This work by Survage goes beyond Cubism, incorporating many of its techniques but also demonstrating a classicism that is timeless.

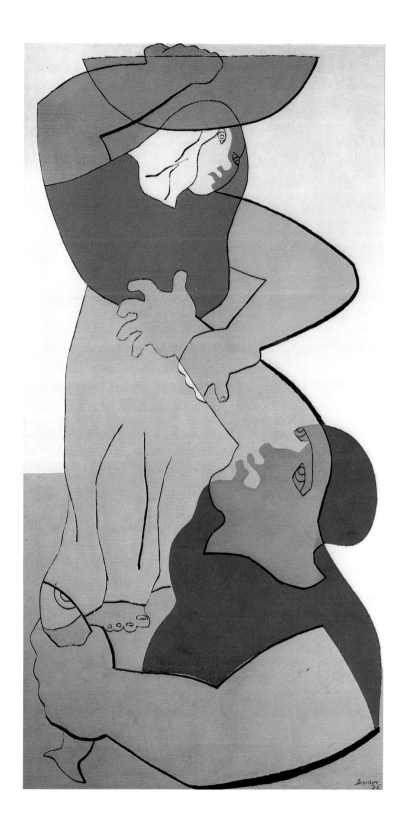

193

Musée du Palais Carnolès, Menton

PAUL DELVAUX

b. Antheit, Belgium, 1897

Maria Serena

1976
Watercolor on paper
55 x 42 cm. (21⅝ x 16½ in.)

Paul Delvaux, the twentieth-century Morpheus, the cartographer of our modern dream-journeys, one of the finest of the contemporary Surrealists, painted his dream-images in the somber language of the somnambulist. Delvaux's women are his hallmark: large-eyed, fragile, with drowned or lost expressions, they populate an extraordinary world of silence, in which motion is suspended and waiting is the only activity.

Delvaux is best known for his powerful and eerie large-size canvases—vivid Surrealist scenarios for dramas of heightened but obscure emotion. However, he is also an incomparable draftsman, and his extensive graphic oeuvre shows a powerful psychology of quite another kind. His drawings and etchings, usually monochromatic or delicately colored in tinted, greyish washes, are filled with the figures of women, sometimes mysterious, sometimes weird or frightening, sometimes, as in the drawing shown here, only gentle and a little frail.

At issue in Delvaux's work is the position of these iconlike women in an identifiable reality. They are drawn in specific (but often unspecified) places, full of the details of everyday life, and hauntingly familiar. Here, *Maria Serena*, the title of the drawing, refers both to the figure and to the room she occupies. In 1976, Delvaux attended the eleventh annual Biennale of Menton, at which he was honored. While there, he stayed in a villa named "Maria Serena," and executed this image of a grave and thoughtful Madonna-like woman.

Delvaux's many sketches and finished drawings are as rich in imagery as his paintings. One can see here, in this drawing of a recognizable place, an example of the way the artist transformed reality into the source-material for his canvases.

194

195

ATTRIBUTED TO ANTONIO MORO

b. Utrecht, ca. 1519
d. Antwerp, 1576

Portrait of a Lady with a Little Dog

1568
Oil on wood
65 x 55 cm. (25%16 x 21⅝ in.)

The formal art of court portraiture was the specialty of Antonio Moro, a favorite painter of Philip II of Spain. Prior to his tenure at Philip's court, he had been the portraitist of the Duke of Alba, the Spanish envoy to the Netherlands. His patrons included Catherine of Portugal, Mary Tudor, and the Cardinal Granvella.

Moro brought to the rather traditional genre of court portraiture a certain lucidity and a lack of idealization that distinguished his work from others'. This fine lady of the Court, dressed in a sober and elegant Spanish style, is portrayed in the realistic, undecorated manner typical of the artist. She is placed against a plain, neutral background, and her features are depicted with a simplicity that does not try to render her unduly beautiful. The small touches of pearls in her hair and jewels at her throat serve to make her generally austere appearance more pronounced.

Portraits of this kind had a rich tradition in the North. Hans Holbein, perhaps the best-known artist of the genre, had made them popular at all the great courts of Europe in the early 1500s. Like Holbein before him, Moro was concerned with accurate portrayal of his sitters. He often placed his figures against a blank ground such as we see here, in order to emphasize their features.

The seriousness and severity of Moro's style had a marked effect on Spanish art, in which a taste for visual veracity and formality in portraiture began to develop at this time.

DONÆ ELBIRA DCHAZ SHIA DIVDGIAE S
DP. DRACA IDD DÑA BEATRIZ DBILL AB AIRIO
FV₁D̄ DIDIo LÃ MSA   D. ILENFST CON
B NÕ. D̄ S . S. AGV   TÍN. AÑ D. 1568.

ATTRIBUTED TO BARTOLMÉ BERMEJO

b. Córdoba, Spain, ca. 1425–30
d. After 1498, place unknown

Portrait of a Nobleman

Undated
Oil on wood
112 x 87 cm. (44¹⁄₁₆ x 34½ in.)

A sojourn in Flanders by Spanish painters was not uncommon in the fifteenth century. The political ties between the two countries were such that a regular cultural commerce existed. Jan van Eyck, the most renowned of the Flemish medieval painters, is thought to have made two trips to Spain, and it is equally likely that Bartolomé Bermejo, the great Spanish master in the Flemish style, travelled to Bruges, where he may have served an apprenticeship under Petrus Christus.

Little else is known of this remarkable painter. His style has much in common with Van Eyck's, but is translated into a distinctly Iberian idiom. The precise detail and rich textures of this portrait (especially in the subtly patterned robe) have a Flemish cast, and the square, expressive face, with its highly individualized features, indicates the extent of Bermejo's training in Bruges. At a time when Spain itself was still little affected by the artistic innovations occurring in Italy, and Spanish art retained the hieratic and programmatic style of the Middle Ages, Bermejo was probably the first Iberian painter to master the Flemish oil-painting technique. His importation of that technique and style to Spain had a great impact there, encouraging the development of realism in color and detail, and initiating a tradition of oil painting that eventually produced Zurbarán and Velázquez.

LUDOVIC BREA

b. Nice, 1450 (?)
d. Nice, 1522/23

Virgin and Child with Saint Francis Kneeling

Undated
Oil on wood
105 x 65 cm. (41⁵⁄₁₆ x 25⁹⁄₁₆ in.)

Ludovic Brea was the founder of a major workshop and atelier in Nice, and the head of a group of artists of the late fifteenth century known as the Niçois Primitives. He was the first to produce works in an indigenously Niçois style, rather than in the Italianate manner. Together with his brother, Antoine, and his nephew, François, he established an early Renaissance Provençal style in Nice and the region of the Côte d'Azur.

Brea and his workshop specialized in the scenes traditional to the period, and popular in the South of France: the Annunciation, the Passion, the Crucifixion, and the Madonna Enthroned. On the whole, his works conform to contemporary and regional taste, rather than being based on the influence of Italy. If an external influence can be detected in this painting, it is, rather, the Flemish, which Ludovic would have assimilated during a sojourn in Genoa, where the Northern style was quite prevalent in the later 1400s. The oval head of the Madonna, and her long, tapering fingers, may be a reference to the art of Flanders. However, the gilded lines in Mary's robe, the sweetness and soft coloring of her and the child's faces, and the hieratic poses of all three figures—holdovers from French medieval style—reflect a distinctly local sensibility.

199

SUZANNE VALADON

b. Bessines, 1865
d. Paris, 1938

Nude Negress

1919
Oil on canvas
160 x 97 cm. (63 x 38³⁄₁₆ in.)

Suzanne Valadon's life fits the classic image of the bohemian artist of *belle époque* Paris. Little is known of her early childhood, except that she was apparently the illegitimate daughter of a laundress and a miller. She lived most of her life in Montmartre; as a girl she worked as an acrobat in a circus. At the age of sixteen, she suffered a fall from a trapeze, and, compelled to leave the circus, became an artist's model. She sat for, among others, Puvis de Chavannes, Renoir, and Degas, and knew most of the artists of the Parisian avant garde. In 1883 she had a child, Maurice Utrillo, who himself became a major artist of the next generation. Valadon had done drawings from an early age, and although she was a close associate of the Symbolists and Impressionists, her art remained independent of their techniques. Toulouse-Lautrec and Degas were perhaps the first to recognize her talent, and her extremely strong sense of line may owe something to them.

Most immediately visible in *Nude Negress* is the presence of a strong temperament. It is a painting from her mature oeuvre; the forcefulness with which it is drawn, the boldness of the figure's pose and expression, and the vividness of the colors all indicate the artistic confidence of the painter. Valadon often painted nudes, usually such strong, hard-edged women. Clearly, this canvas takes some of its exotic flavor from the example of Gauguin (whose *Annah the Javanese* of 1893–94 is a remarkably similar treatment of the nude), just as the sureness with which the black outlines of the figure are set down may reflect her association with Lautrec and Degas. But Valadon's work is distinctive for its sharp clarity and realism in the modern idiom—at a time when modernism had taken the route of abstraction. Perhaps the most arresting feature of this canvas is that the face, with its firm black brows, short chin, and sharp nose, bears a close resemblance to that of the artist. Most of Valadon's canvases are domestic scenes; the bold primitivism of this painting, and its unusual theme, give us an unusual insight into her remarkable personality.

201

FRANCOIS DESNOYER

b. Montauban, 1894
d. Perpignan, 1972

The "Pointe Courte" at Sète

1955
Oil on canvas
176 x 114 cm. (69⁵⁄₁₆ x 44⅞ in.)

The town of Sète, on the Côte d'Azur, has attracted artists since the turn of the century. Like many of the small coastal towns, it has a colorful port, of the kind that the Fauves, among others, loved to paint. François Desnoyer came to live in Sète in 1945, and painted scenes of the port often. (Albert Marquet's treatment of the same view, done in 1920, is reproduced on page 47 of this volume.)

Desnoyer was a friend of Gromaire and Villon, and a member of the French avant garde of the period between the two world wars. Influenced by the Fauves in his use of color (a characteristic of much painting done in the South of France is a brilliant, light-filled palette) and by the Cubists in his careful, geometrical structuring of his compositions, Desnoyer was nevertheless a rather classical artist, with a strong sense of perspective, of gesture, and of imagination. The generation of painters that flowered after World War I was concerned with the concept of space and form within the canvas, on and beneath the picture plane. Their experiments in the use of color independent of form, and in compressed and expanded perspective, brought many of them to the brink of abstraction and some, beyond. In this painting, Desnoyer's concern to reconcile these experiments with a traditional, almost academic, topic can be seen. The picture is densely packed with forms: in the foreground, boats are stacked virtually one on top of another, as are the sheds in the upper part of the canvas. Yet above these, a sky of traditional blue, paling to white at the horizon, creates a conventional sense of landscape distance in a manner that can be traced back to Piero della Francesca and the Umbrian Renaissance. The colors in general are cheerful and bold, applied in a heavy impasto, but only sometimes depart from the naturalistic; the figures are for the most part flesh-colored, the water of the harbor is blue, except where reflections from surrounding buildings strike it. Only in subtle touches—a pink window, another painted bright blue—does the artist employ the technique of the Fauves. The strength of this painting lies in Desnoyer's confident choice of vivid colors, the tight composition, and the deft boldness with which lines and planes are set down—all skills to be found as much in the Renaissance as in the twentieth century.

ALBERT GLEIZES

b. Paris, 1881
d. St.-Rémy, 1953

Painting for Contemplation

1932
Oil on canvas
141 x 111 cm. (55½ x 43¹¹⁄₁₆ in.)

Albert Gleizes was one of the central theoreticians of Cubism. Together with Jean Metzinger and Robert Delaunay, he developed the formal and structural principles on which Cubism is based—an achievement that paralleled the work of Picasso and Braque.

In 1910, when Gleizes's forceful style was beginning to emerge, Picasso and Braque had begun painting in the Analytical Cubist manner. The original intent of Cubism, as they saw it, was to explore, analyze, and describe an object in space in terms of form, but without adhering to conventional principles of perspective. Thus, the image of an object was created monochromatically, in terms of its planes, lines, and shape, avoiding overt spiritual content. Gleizes and Delaunay, though working in close contact with Picasso, Braque, and their circle, used the Cubist technique to quite another end. Less interested in purely visual problems, they, Gleizes especially, desired to fill their canvases with images of greater emotional impact. In particular, Gleizes wanted to express the passage of time, motion, space, and the infinite variety of elements in the visible world. Like the Analytical Cubists, he broke down objects into distinct planes, but in contrast to them, emphasized the energy and emotional response such images could excite. He sought to depict the great themes of harmony and evolution.

In 1912, Gleizes published a book entitled *Cubism* with Metzinger. In it they said: "The picture bears its pretext, the reason for its existence, within it. . . . It does not harmonize with this or that environment; it harmonizes with things in general, with the universe: it is an organism." Gradually, this notion of the organic quality of art evolved into a concept of the universe as an organic entity, represented in art through abstract, harmonious images. Gleizes's ideals, and his use of color and form to express action, motion, and harmony, brought him very close to Kandinsky, who was pursuing similar concerns at this time.

By the 1930s—the period in which this canvas was painted—Gleizes's art had become somewhat less agitated; it took on a cool, more calculated tone, such as we see here, and, while it continued to represent visually a concept of emotional harmony, it did so with less excitement. The title of *Painting for Contemplation* indicates this change in sentiment. Smooth, unmodulated areas of color are counterpointed by equal areas of checkerboards and dots; soft pastels are punctuated by pure primary colors—vivid reds and blues. The composition, a rectangle enclosing a ring, which in turn encloses a small, nearly centered oval of black, is based on a highly geometrical ideal of balance, form, and order, and is designed to evoke a sense of repose.

GRAHAM SUTHERLAND

b. London, 1903
d. London, 1980

The Fountain

1966
Oil on canvas
145 x 123 cm. (57 1/16 x 48 7/16 in.)

In his later years, Graham Sutherland owned a house at Menton, where he spent several months each summer, painting in the famous light of the Côte d'Azur. Sutherland's art, like that of Henry Moore and Francis Bacon, evolved in England in the 1930s and 1940s and gained its full strength during World War II. Like Bacon and Moore, he was occupied throughout his life with representational art, with the response of the artist to nature and its images. In his canvases, nature figures as a great force with the power to transform or distort; Sutherland's universe is populated with the creatures and spirits deformed by that power.

Certain natural images recur in his paintings: rocks; small animals such as birds, toads, stag beetles, and mantises; hybrid creatures suggestive of a variety of plants and animals, called "horned forms"; and repeated water images—fountains, waterfalls, canals, cisterns, rivers, and estuaries. In these pictures, paint is laid on in thick brushstrokes that have a highly organic quality, almost a life of their own. The objects seem to metamorphose from animal to plant to mineral within each canvas, implying a unity between the different forms of nature and an intermingling of the natural with the mechanistic.

Here, the *Fountain* sprouts leaves, fleshy shapes, objects that look like eyes, and mechanical parts. It is one in a series on the fountain theme done between 1964 and 1966. In these paintings, with their tenebrous images, strong painterly style, and rich evocation of organic forms, Sutherland presents a view of the physical or material world that is mysterious but not abstract, eerie but not surrealistic. His images of this period are, rather, a metaphor for the ambiguous and changing condition of the world.

Index of Artists

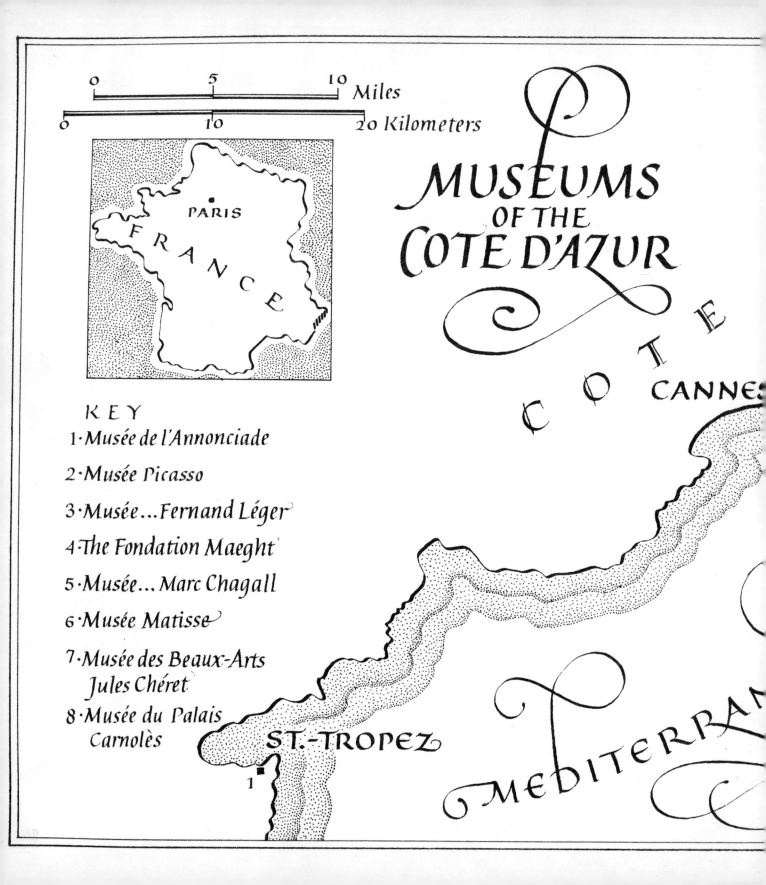

MUSEUMS
OF THE
COTE D'AZUR

CÔTE

CANNES

KEY

1·Musée de l'Annonciade

2·Musée Picasso

3·Musée...Fernand Léger

4·The Fondation Maeght

5·Musée...Marc Chagall

6·Musée Matisse

7·Musée des Beaux-Arts
Jules Chéret

8·Musée du Palais
Carnolès

PARIS

FRANCE

0   5   10   Miles

0   10   20   Kilometers

ST.-TROPEZ

MEDITERRAN

1